The Ancient Story of God-With-Us

The Ancient Story of God-With-Us

RAY C. ROBLES

foreword by Mark Chironna

CASCADE *Books* • Eugene, Oregon

THE ANCIENT STORY OF GOD-WITH-US

Copyright © 2025 Ray C. Robles. All rights reserved. Except for brief quotations in critical publications or reviews, no part of this book may be reproduced in any manner without prior written permission from the publisher. Write: Permissions, Wipf and Stock Publishers, 199 W. 8th Ave., Suite 3, Eugene, OR 97401.

Cascade Books
An Imprint of Wipf and Stock Publishers
199 W. 8th Ave., Suite 3
Eugene, OR 97401

www.wipfandstock.com

PAPERBACK ISBN: 979-8-3852-0341-3
HARDCOVER ISBN: 979-8-3852-0342-0
EBOOK ISBN: 979-8-3852-0343-7

Cataloguing-in-Publication data:

Names: Robles, Ray C., author.

Title: The ancient story of God-with-us / Ray C. Robles.

Description: Eugene, OR: Cascade Books, 2025 | Includes bibliographical references and index.

Identifiers: ISBN 979-8-3852-0341-3 (paperback) | ISBN 979-8-3852-0342-0 (hardcover) | ISBN 979-8-3852-0343-7 (ebook)

Subjects: LCSH: Bible—Criticism, interpretation, etc. | Creedal Christianity. | Trinity—History of doctrines.

Classification: BT111.3 R60 2025 (paperback) | BT111.3 (ebook)

VERSION NUMBER 04/04/25

Scripture quotations are from New Revised Standard Version Bible, copyright © 1989 National Council of the Churches of Christ in the United States of America. Used by permission. All rights reserved worldwide.

Para los pioneros de mi historia con Dios:
Luis Martinez, Alfonsa Martinez, César Robles, y Ana Robles

Contents

Foreword by Mark Chironna | *ix*

Acknowledgments | *xi*

Introduction | *xiii*

PART I	(Re)Interpreting the World	1
Chapter 1	Filters of Knowing	3
Chapter 2	Our Storied Reality	12
Chapter 3	Speaking of God	20
Chapter 4	The God Who Moves History	31
Chapter 5	The Spirited Testimony of Jesus	39
PART II	The Myths That Have Severed God from Creatures	57
Chapter 6	A Fitting Place for God	59
Chapter 7	The God Who Refuses Safe Distances	71
Chapter 8	Out with the Old, Forward with the Ancient	90

Conclusion | *109*

Bibliography | *113*

General Index | *117*

Scripture Index | *121*

Foreword

Dr. Ray Robles is a dear friend and a trusted voice for our time, and in "The Ancient Story Of God-With-Us," he offers a fresh and needed perspective for navigating the challenges many of us face in our faith today. For so many of us, the frameworks we inherited, while sincere, have left us feeling unprepared to engage the complexity of the world around us. Yet, in a moment when so much of culture—and even faith—leans toward deconstruction, leaving people spiritually adrift, Ray reminds us that there is another way to journey forward.

He calls us to rediscover the richness of the Christian tradition—not as a rigid system of rules, but as a living and dynamic conversation that has carried the church through centuries of change and challenge. Christianity is far more than rigid ideology; it is a rich and living tradition with room to grow and explore faithfully, while holding fast to the truth of the Gospel.

Ray doesn't write at us but with us, walking alongside as a fellow pilgrim who understands both the weariness of disillusionment and the joy of rediscovery. This book doesn't offer surface-level solutions but calls us to explore the deep waters of our faith with courage and trust. It challenges us to root ourselves in the wisdom of the church's history while remaining alive to the Spirit's work in our time. It's a reminder that the God who has sustained His people through upheaval and trial is still present and calling us into a faith that is both anchored in history and alive to his Spirit today.

For those of us who have felt tired, disillusioned, or uncertain about where to go next in our walk with Christ, this book offers hope. It reminds us that we don't have to bear the weight of figuring it all out alone. There is a reservoir of grace and wisdom from which the church has drawn throughout its history—and one that remains available to us today.

As a friend and fellow sojourner, I wholeheartedly commend this book to you. It is a timely, thoughtful, and challenging work that will inspire you to remain grounded in the tradition of our faith while responding to the fresh invitation of God's Spirit.

Bishop Mark J. Chironna, PhD

Acknowledgments

THIS BOOK MAKES A BIG deal out of how crucial relationships are to personal identity. As such, I must celebrate the relationships that have made me who I am and have also shaped the writing of this book.

My soulmate, Christina. We have lived so much life together that it's impossible to distinguish my own life from yours (nor would I want to). I still remember sitting in my office so long ago, despairing because I was certain that I was wasting my time thinking and laboring about the things of God that I thought would never resonate with anyone. You hugged me while I was down there on the floor and assured me that God was calling me to do this despite the hidden season I was in, then demanded that I get up and apologize to myself and my work. There have been many such moments. It is because of your unrelenting support that I am who I am today.

To my little Jiu Jitsu star, Marlon. I love your dance moves, your original riddles, your love for science experiments, your overall talent at everything you try, your hilarious sense of humor, and your endless affection. Thank you for giving me the coolest title I have: Marlon's dad.

Mom and Dad, I still can't say enough about your generosity. Your endless support, intercessory prayers, and belief in me have far exceeded your call as parents. Thank you for raising me in the ways of God, even when that meant insisting that I go to church at least four times a week throughout my childhood. Templo Bethesda is with me forever as are my tíos and tías who have made it all but impossible for me to be anything other than Christian.

ACKNOWLEDGMENTS

Thank you, and I love you all. To my in-laws: you've provided us with love and a piece of heaven that is the farm as a place for solitude, healing, writing, and play!

Thank you to my students at GCU for allowing me many opportunities to discipline my theology-speak to make it understandable. Conversations with you have helped shape the way that I wrote this book. To my dear friends and peers in ministry. You all have spoken into my life at various crucial moments: D. A. Sherron, Mark Chironna, Onaje Jefferson, Moises Felipé, Daniel Medeiros, Ken Mitchell, Chris Green, Harif Hazera, Jordan Francis, and many others. Also, to the team of precious people laboring alongside Christina and me for the seed and the dream known as Archetype Church. Your steadfastness, intercession, and love have sustained us in more ways than you know. We couldn't do it without you all. Heart Worship Collective, it has been a joy not only to pour into the vision of the Jefferson family, but to receive in kind. Thank you all for being the answer to our family's deepest prayers for community. Let's all keep it pushing for the kingdom. The best is yet to come.

Lydia Neeley, I think you have one of the toughest jobs in this book writing process as you are the first line of defense between my thoughts and the eyes of the public! It's no easy task separating the wheat from the chaff in my writing, and you have bravely done so for the last two projects with precision and excellence. Thank you.

Introduction

I pray that you may have the power to comprehend, with all the saints, what is the breadth and length and height and depth, and to know the love of Christ that surpasses knowledge, so that you may be filled with all the fullness of God.

—Ephesians 3:18–19

When I talk to my Christian university students who are serious about their faith, I notice a common tension. On the one hand, they have a sincere desire to be faithful in a world where it feels to them like truth is constantly being challenged. For them, faithfulness is found in following the conventions given to them by their parents, families, pastors, and favorite online Christian commentators. Rightly, they want to maintain these visions in a world seemingly gone mad, and any attempt to nudge them, even slightly, in a direction other than the "straight and narrow" as received from their contexts is met with deep suspicion at best, and a disdained rejection at worst.

On the other hand, there is also a quiet, yet increasing recognition that something is amiss with what they have received. They don't know exactly what it is, much less how to navigate their way around it. They're not interested in total deconstruction, but neither does the option of business as usual resonate for them. They can deeply feel the anxiety-inducing problems of the world where change is constant and novelty reigns supreme. They want to resist it, but how? As I will discuss early on in this book, finding a Bible verse here and there to combat these tensions is not in any way a sustaining help. Nor will the distant God "up there," who mostly looks at us while intermittently "intervening" in history, suffice. They believe in God, but wonder, how does he actually make himself available to us in a "natural" world that is seemingly made to get on without him? God seems to reside serenely up there, while we undergo the madness of this changing world down here.

As you will see in this book, I am convinced that the future of the church involves becoming deeply rooted in our ancient faith while also remaining attuned to the Spirit of the living God. The first part, the seeking of deeper roots, will involve a creative retrieval of our ancient and enchanted Christian tradition. It's already happening, and I have been witnessing its captivating power firsthand. Indeed, I have been witnessing more and more students visiting churches that honor the ancient practices with more frequency. Much of this has to do with their novelty fatigue. Living in a reactionary world that forms you to seek new trends has grown quite stale and exhausting. Where can I be grounded? There's too much pressure to sustain my own relationship with Jesus through my private effort of reading and prayer. There's also too much pressure on me as an individual to keep the passion and fire ignited. So then, what book of the Bible should I read? What should I be feeling when I do? Why pray? Why does God feel so distant? I'm tired.

With questions like these, I never seek to push them into a particular denominational expression. Frankly, I think they're a bit disenchanted by such rigidity, but haven't been shown an alternative option aside from those which seem to want to push them away from all conviction and all truth. Again, these students *want* to be faithful. But what do we do when our inherited vision leaves us feeling cold, and has quietly done so for a very long time? I mentioned in the previous paragraph that the future of the church will also involve attunement to God's presentness. So then, what do we do when we're having dreams of God visiting us, speaking to us, and encountering us when we've had no mental furniture to know what to do with such encounters? This is indeed happening with these students at a very high rate, and beyond them.

INTRODUCTION

I've had many in my office asking me what to do. What's more, I know this is not something unique to these younger generations. People of all ages have been dealing with this. The conversations, when honest and vulnerable, tend to push in the direction of being deeply rooted in a faith that has been here long before we, or our denominations, have. And if you have an interest in this book, I trust this is the case for you as well.

A big aim of this book is to show Christian readers in America and beyond that the term *Christian* names a tradition that is far more expansive than our denominational and Western mindsets have understood. It is simply not so that your inherited denomination thinks the way that they do because they're the only ones who still take the Bible seriously, and that everyone else would think exactly like your denominational officials if only they took the Bible as seriously as they do. This fantasy is becoming more impossible to maintain.

Having said that, what are some strategies for how to receive a vision of the Christian faith that resonates with your deep desires, is emphatically Christian, but feels so strange to your conventional thinking? I suggest that an important step is to recognize the difference between a tradition and an ideology. Christianity is a tradition. Traditions can withstand the shifting sands of culture worldwide and throughout millennia because they don't crumble from critique (including "deconstruction"). Traditions are roomy and sturdy enough to develop their thought throughout time while remaining true to themselves. It took Christianity centuries of wrestling with how Father, Son, and Spirit could be equally God (a core Christian dogma), with various faulty ideas being taught along the way. Yet, Christianity remained because part of what it means to be a tradition is to be part of an ongoing conversation—not to be afraid of it.

What's considered dogma in the Christian tradition is incredibly minimal. Take for example what has become a hot-button issue like modern understandings of the doctrine of creation. Read the creeds and you will see that all we must believe is that God is creator. How does God create, or "in how many days," or how "long ago" did it happen? There's room for conversation because there's no Christian dogma on the dates or the "how" questions. Or, an even bigger issue that has caused fierce division, what is the nature of Jesus's "return?" Will there be a literal millennium, a rapture, a literal tribulation? I can affirm one or none of these and still be Christian. For all that Christian dogma says is that I must believe about the end is that "Jesus Christ . . . will come again to judge the living and dead." That's what the Christian *tradition* affords us: the opportunity to be part of an ongoing conversation and remain Christian despite some variances. So, when I talk about God, or deem something a "central issue," I must bear this in mind.

Contrastingly, ideologies cannot stomach such roominess. Once a slight nuance is detected, out come the inquisitors and gatekeepers. The reason why ideologies are so incredibly rigid with strict boundaries that must be protected is precisely because of how fragile they are. "Slippery slopes" threaten ideologies at every side. Thus, they cannot withstand anything other than enthusiastic affirmations to all their propositional tenets. It is no surprise, then, that in the horizon of history, ideologies are relatively short-lived as they are mostly sustained by the commonsensical conventions of culture that support them. Once convention changes, they're forced to change with it, or die. The same goes for the ideologies whose entire identity is rooted in emphatic resistance to culture. Indeed, fundamentalism is as much a modern phenomenon as is unreflective cultural assimilation.

This book will demonstrate that, thanks be to God, Christianity is a tradition and not an ideology. I emphatically love the church. I am aware that it has become popular to rebuke this or that church, and this or that preacher while also noting this or that major scandal as what's wrong with Christians today. Those critiques are legitimate albeit obvious, and the church has much to repent from. However, in this book, I have in mind the people in popular church contexts who still love the church despite being rightly disillusioned, and perhaps may not be quite sure how to answer the question, "Where do we go from here?"

INTRODUCTION

This book, I hope, will give the good news that you do not have to bear this burden and think your way out of this all by yourself. Christianity is an ancient tradition that has withstood much worse—in terms of scandal, division, bad political leaders, social upheaval, false teaching—and has remained itself throughout two thousand years in both the East and the West. We, the church, have been here before. In fact, we have been through much worse, and yet the gates of hell shall not prevail against us.

Indeed, the gates of hell shall not prevail against the universal church, but insofar as our personal churches are captive to behaving like ideologies, there's no promise of prevailing. Denominations that cling to rigidity may die, and perhaps time will tell whether that is a good thing. For now, it is my prayer that if you have been disillusioned by a version of Christianity that feels stale, lonely, exhausting, mind-numbing, uninspired, arid, and hopelessly political, that you recognize that you can still be Christian while seeking to be reenchanted by the God of wonder. The ancient Christian tradition gives us deep wells from which to draw again and again, wooing us deeper into the inexhaustible mystery of the triune God-with-us. Come on in, the water is fine.

PART I

(Re)Interpreting the World

THIS BOOK HAS TWO distinct parts. In contrast to the dull back-and-forth state of either trying to be relevant, or viscerally reacting against such attempts, in Part I, I am working from the assumption that the church does in fact have a unique and compelling way of being in the world. It is a vision that has been developing for millennia, and it has thrived through various kingdoms, cultures, and institutions across time. The church claims to know the Lord of history who has acted among us to reconstruct the world at large, and therefore, his acts also reconstruct what it means to be human. These are not boring claims; they're audacious.

Given this audacious self-understanding of the people of God, the church has consistently recognized its need to be communally formed. There have always been competing visions of human identity, religious identity, theology, and the good life. These competing worldly visions don't come merely by way of ideas, but through images, advertising, and practices. The church has known this, and so the church has labored to create its own practices, habits, and ways of speaking that embody a very ancient story that is still being told and lived today. When we lose touch with the church's ancient way of being in the world, we lose touch with its way of thinking in the world. Part I, then, is an attempt to retrieve the church's ancient self-understanding in a way that the modern Christian can receive as an identity-forming gift. Whatever you imagine to be an insurmountable problem for the church, we have been through much worse in our history, and have not only sojourned out of it, but have thrived through it. That said, it is worth our efforts to draw from this ancient wisdom.

In the first five chapters that make up Part I, I aim to retrieve the centrality of community, story, and the ancient Christian vision of triune God-with-us for the sake of moving forward in our history as God's people. This is not about being nostalgic but moving forward faithfully. That said, I also account for the work of the Holy Spirit who is the lively and transformative presence of God in our midst. The Spirit of God does not merely help us recall the past but surprises us as he calls us to live from the future he intends for creatures. Therefore, I will also pay careful attention to the Holy Spirit's work in the biblical story. The Holy Spirit joins us to God, to each other, and to our shared story's final fulfillment in the life of the triune God.

Understanding the depths of who we are as creatures and as Christians is wholly dependent upon pursuing the truth of who our creator, the triune God, is. Part I is not just about who we are, but about who, and indeed *what* the triune God is. There is no knowing of God that isn't also a knowing of his story with his creatures. This will be a driving thought as we wade through the ancient story of God-with-us.

CHAPTER 1

Filters of Knowing

If we assume we are each of us a world to ourselves, we end up alienated from the destiny of others.

—ROWAN WILLIAMS

After all, what is a person other than a whole history of associations, loves, memories, attachments, and affinities? Who are we, other than all the others who have made us who we are, and to whom we belong as much as they to us?

—DAVID BENTLEY HART

KNOWING OURSELVES

I have found that one of the more illuminating lessons for the young students who fill my lecture halls revolves around a simple but profound musing from a German-Jewish philosopher named Edith Stein, who died in the Holocaust in 1942. She was a brilliant thinker who once quipped that she found it very philosophically interesting that she couldn't see the back of her head while everyone else could. The key idea here is that it's impossible to fully know herself, all by herself. Put differently, she can only know herself *fully* in relationship to other people.

Of course, this sounds offensive for our culturally hyper-individualistic tendencies. But, as I often point out, if it were true that we could indeed know ourselves all by ourselves, then a prisoner coming out of solitary confinement could plausibly walk out of his punishment enlightened. But as the data shows, the opposite is the case. By and large, they tend to go mad, or at least be pushed to the brink of it. Some never recover. It would seem, then, that the antidote to going mad is recognizing that one's sanity, and one's true personal humanity, depends on *rightly relating to others* and vice versa. The biblical word for this is *righteousness*: rightly relating to God in rightly relating to others.

Knowing myself truly, then, is a matter of embracing the relationships that rightly form me. For example, I know myself as the grandson of my maternal grandparents Luis and Alfonsa, my paternal grandparents César and Ana, the son of César and Hilda, the nephew of fourteen aunts and uncles, and a cousin to forty-plus relatives. I know myself as the husband of Christina, the father of Marlon, and friend of many. Furthermore, I know myself as a theology teacher and writer, formed by my interactions with students and colleagues. I also have been taught by various women and men in Sunday school, from the pulpit, lecture halls, seminars, and all the authors from the books read therein. Furthermore, all those people described above have their own families, friends, colleagues, and other relationships that have formed them, which consequently shape how they engage me. The simple but foundational point here is that we are all inescapably bound to one other for the sake of knowing ourselves truly and fully. To put it more directly and technically: we are not isolated beings; rather, we are beings-in-relation.

On the negative side we have all sinned against others and have also been sinned against by others. As a result, we have tendencies to *wrongly relate to others* or be wrongly related to. This is what it means to live unrighteously. It means that I fail to live rightly before God by failing to live rightly with others. Considering the prevalence of unrighteous relationships, to know myself rightly is also a matter of rejecting or setting serious boundaries on those relationships that aren't good for me, nor I for them. If I resist the influence of my manipulators or abusers, the healing process is not completed with my isolation from all interaction. Rather, in the process of healing, I slowly receive a new task of vulnerability on my life: a search for a new way of being that will inevitably be a quest to find different people that I feel I can relate to. This tends to be the case whether I leave a church, a family, or a group due to abuses suffered at their hands. For better or worse, we are created to live as beings-in-relation. The aim then is to live in right relation with one another, and therefore with God. Then, and only then, can I truly know myself.

KNOWING GOD

As impossible as it is to imagine knowing myself all by myself, even more impossible still is trying to imagine knowing God without human relationships and influence. I didn't find God by myself any more than I "found" the Spanish and English languages by myself. I speak the way I do because I was first spoken to by those related to me. So also, God was first spoken *to* me through others. God grasped me by first introducing himself to my grandparents through those who formed them. Later my grandparents became pastors on my maternal side, and evangelists/pastors on my paternal side. They started churches in which my parents were formed to understand who God is, and so on. I am a product of these churches. I grew up in a Spanish-speaking church, living in the United States in the twentieth and twenty-first centuries in a Puerto Rican and Mexican family headed by Christian leaders. Growing up this way and in this time meant that my family inherited certain understandings of who God is from their broader context. They also inherited ways of reading Scripture that were celebrated as faithful within said context. These values were passed on to me, implicitly and explicitly. Just so, I was given a context and a vantage from which to make sense of the world, as we all are. Whether you are aware or not, you too were given a common sense, a context, or a framework for engaging God and reading Scripture that tells you what questions are worth asking and what methods are best in discerning the truth. I will say a bit more about this in the next section.

Knowing God and knowing ourselves cannot be completely separated from knowing others. Appealing to a direct relationship with God and asserting confidently that "I get my identity from God, and God alone" won't do. When the narrative of Scripture notes the encounter of an individual with God, it is always done for the sake of a call to a community, and that community is called for the sake of the world. "Go," says God to Abram, "to the Land that I will show you. I will make of you a great nation, and I will bless you and make your name great, so that you will be a blessing" (Gen 12:1–2). God goes on to say later that "by your offspring shall all the nations of the earth gain blessing for themselves, for you have obeyed my voice" (Gen 22:18). The voice of God for one is ultimately for the sake of the many. The stage for our call to communal existence has already been set even earlier in the biblical narrative. In the seemingly ideal conditions of a blissful garden, Adam was with God alone and God said, "It is not good that man should be alone" (Gen 2:18). This is one thing that is proclaimed as "not good" before the fall and so God created another for Adam to relate to, which would yield a larger community tasked with the blessing of others. Their disobedience to God immediately yielded unrighteous living with one another through scapegoating and blame-shifting. When we put our individualistic context aside, then, we will begin to see that the story of Scripture is not about me and God, but about God with *us*.

A key to knowing God and myself is also knowing the "us" that I am a part of. It's the "us" that Scripture is primarily concerned with, in service to creation at large. Yet, today what we celebrate as good discipleship—that is, overemphasizing private prayer, devotion, private Bible reading, and spending time with God alone—can be understood as re-creating the early conditions of the garden, which God said was not good. Those conditions were of just one isolated person communing with God. Privately communing with God is not bad per se. Even Jesus would retreat to be with the Father. But, when it is celebrated as the high point of daily evangelical piety, something alien to the Christian faith and more at home in modern individualism starts to take shape. It starts to look like: just me and God, just me and my Bible. If this goes unchecked, it can result in misconstruing others as a threat to your understanding of God and Scripture. It creates a world where Christians are never worried about their own blind spots, and so view the motives of other Christians who disagree with them as suspect, so that a slight disagreement leads to a split. This is anti-community made possible by overestimating my individual ability to be faithful all by myself. Claiming that individuals can know themselves and God all by themselves is not only mistaken, but it also cripples the process of communal discernment that is needed to lead us out of deception for the sake of moving us closer to truth.

KNOWING WITH OTHERS

If you grew up in the Western world, specifically and especially, if you grew up in America, there is a very good chance that before you met or encountered God personally, you knew *of* him. Even if you were not raised in a family that explicitly served God, you grew up around church buildings, logos adorned with crosses, vague references to God on our currency or in the Pledge of Allegiance, popular culture, and award shows. God has, in many ways, already gone through a variety of filters before penetrating your inner life and imagination.

Filters of knowing God through humans and the inherited philosophies of the day are inescapable. The aim isn't to do away with other humans to get to the "real God." Christianity does not give us that option. For Christians, humans can be both the problem and the solution in getting to know God, but they cannot be done away with. A unique feature of Christianity is that we as his followers do not possess any direct writings from our founder himself. Think about it. Jesus did not directly write anything that we as his followers read and study. So how, then, do we know what he said and did? Through other people. Indeed, there's no access to the teachings and life of Jesus without the writings from the human hands of Matthew, Mark, Luke, John, Paul, etc. We don't have the writings of Jesus or his personal journal to chronicle his life; we only have what others told us he said and did, and trusting their witness is how we know God.

Without human witnesses, then, I would not be a Christian. Indeed, part of what it looks like to be Christian is to have the discernment and faith to recognize that Matthew telling me about Jesus is coequal with Jesus himself speaking to me. That's why the Bible, although written by the hands of human authors, can, in some sense, be called the word of God. To take it one last step further, my dependency on human beings is not limited to the writers of Scripture alone, for I also wouldn't have the Bible itself if not for other people (i.e., the church) recognizing the breath of God on these texts. The historic church then gathered them and gifted them to others. Throughout history, the passing down of these writings made their way to my family, and then to me.

KNOWING IN CONTEXT

I briefly mentioned earlier that everyone is given a context from which to understand the world, God, and Christian Scriptures, whether we are aware of it or not. I will continue that point in more detail here. Considering that the most basic things we know about God, his relationship to creation, and Scripture, are embedded into our imaginations through our relationships even before we learn how to think deeply about such things, it becomes an ever-important task to bring these presuppositions to light. The irony here is that the more and the longer we ignore presuppositions, the stronger their grip on our collective imaginations. Moreover, the more invisible they are to us, the more powerful their influence.

Presuppositions don't just teach us how to answer important questions, they tell us what questions are worth asking. For example, something I will be talking about throughout the course of this book is that we have lost touch with talking and thinking about God—the very being of God—in our current American Christian imagination, and more specifically, we have neglected talking about *what* God is. Not finding God-talk to be all that important is, to my judgment, a very bad presupposition that we need to recognize and heal for the sake of a better future of the American church. As it stands, the doctrine of the Trinity tends to evoke for many Christians in this context nothing more than a shrug of our shoulders. This haphazard appeal to "mystery" happens not just for regular folks who attend church, but also for pastors. How can this be if we're talking about the very God around whom we as Christians claim to center our lives? We fall prey to this blissful apathy not because these questions are historically unimportant for Christians, but because our recently inherited version of Christianity tells us that different questions are more important.

As I will show in greater detail later, this is at least partially due to the fact that we have primarily engaged God for the last several hundred years obsessing over a topic that has shaped how we understand God, how we build and participate in church, and how we read Scripture. That topic centers around particular understandings of "salvation," removed from concern of identifying the triune God who acts in our midst. "Salvation" in our popular imagination is rooted in trying to understand simple models for how God saves individual people. For some pastors, that's the only question worth asking. Therefore, "theology" collapses into memorizing and stacking biblical prooftexts or memory verses around doctrines of salvation removed from the narrative that identifies him. From here, questions emerge like: Which individuals are "saved" (read: going to heaven), and which are not? What techniques can we employ to ensure we are "in" and not "out"? How does God "save" individuals? Do individuals contribute to their salvation at all? In our inherited context, these questions have determined what we look for in Scripture.

Also, notice how the word "God" in the question "how does *God* save individuals?" is taken for granted. We presuppose that we know who God is without hesitation and move right into asking how he saves. This is relatively new for the two thousand years of Christian thought. Even early Christians who had vibrant devotional and intimate lives with God didn't imagine that they knew him in a way that they could just assume they knew his essence and move on to other topics. Rather, other theological topics were completely wrapped up in the question of who this God is. Christian thinkers and worshippers, for at least the first millennium and a half of their existence, were consumed by this question. Who and "what" is God? It permeated their prayer life, worship life, thought life, communal life. Hence their spirituality was shaped by and around the God who was named Father, Son, and Holy Spirit.

Today, we tend to bypass that question altogether. We assume we "know" who he is without much need for reflection. Imagining that knowing God is either simple and obvious, or so mysterious it's not worth the effort, we evade the problem by jumping right to questions about individual salvation. When these salvation questions permeate the Christian imagination as strongly as they have for the past few centuries, it shapes our communal and individual self-understanding. It tells us how to "do" church, missions, and read Scripture. It's a vicious cycle.

Hence, evangelical Christians have been stuck on this teeter totter. As of now, one side insists that church should be relevant. After all, if all that matters is that "God saves from eternal torment" then our messaging ought to be attractive to the culture so as to draw people to come to church to increase their opportunity for "getting saved." "No!" Say the others. "God saves sovereignly and the relevant approach waters down the gospel." For the latter, real church and true Christianity is about teaching through books of the Bible while making sure we preach hard against sin and remain passionate about holiness and mission. So, the excruciating back and forth between those two visions and their variants continue. Whether a teeter totter or a pendulum, I want off this ride. Neither does the truth lie in the "balance" or "somewhere in the middle" between these two options. To be frank, I find these discussions to be rather boring and utterly mistaken. Yet, we remain here nonetheless, and I will later trace how we ended up here and map a way out.

Conclusion

This leads us to one last major thread of what makes up our identities as beings-in-relation, or beings-in-community. Story. As I will note in the following chapter, story is the glue that holds our personal and communal identities intact. Without story there is no community. Without a storied community, there is no personal identity. While I only know myself in relationship with other people, we know ourselves by the stories that animate our lives both individually and communally. Where are we from? Where are we heading? Who are we? Where do I fit within the "we"? To answer this, we turn to story in more detail. More specifically, the Christian story.

In summary:

1. Our personal identities are not self-made but are formed by and how we relate to others.
2. Just as I cannot bypass others to know myself, neither can I simply bypass others in my knowing of God.
3. Therefore, community is necessary in knowing both myself and God.
4. Communities are animated by the *story* they understand themselves to be a part of. To be part of the community as a contributing member is to know and live according to the story.

CHAPTER 2

Our Storied Reality

I can only answer the question "What am I to do?" if I can answer the prior question "Of what story of stories do I find myself a part?"

—ALASDAIR MACINTYRE, *AFTER VIRTUE*

THE MADNESS OF CHANGE

LONG AGO, AROUND 500 BC, there was a man who went by the name Heraclitus. He was a philosopher whose thoughts could drive a sane person mad. This is exactly what ended up happening to one of his disciples who went by the name Cratylus. Cratylus attempted to live solely by the philosophy of his teacher. Ultimately, he stopped talking based on principle. This was odd. Cratylus was not the victim of a bad accident that disabled his vocal cords. He simply fell silent to remain true to the philosophy he held. When he was hungry, he would not speak, but wag his finger for someone to bring him food. A once sane man who did not lose his ability to speak had stopped speaking. Why would a person voluntarily live in such a state of madness? What was the underpinning philosophy of such a life?

Well, his teacher Heraclitus claimed that nothing exists except change. Change happens to everything, everywhere, all the time. Nothing stays steady and unchanged long enough to exist.

Here one second, changed and gone in the next. Nothing simply exists. For Cratylus, living by this philosophy meant that silence was the only way to live in accordance with reality. Why? Because for words to have meaning, they must refer to *something*. However, since nothing exists because everything is changing, there's nothing there to talk about. Words don't refer to anything at all. They are just noise coming out of the front of your head, and people who are to be respected don't just make noise. Better to stay silent.

For Heraclitus, then, life can be understood as ever-changing people, places, and things going through a meaningless succession of events. One fleeting moment is followed by another, and then another, and on it goes until we die. This, of course, is not a Christian option, and yet Christians today have been just as susceptible to these ideas as is our world. As ancient as Heraclitus and Cratylus are, the philosophy they lived by is still alive and well. The madness and anxieties we feel as our lives are constantly in flux are the fruit of our society unwittingly living by Heraclitus's principles. Everything is constant change. Everything is disconnected, meaningless, and an un-storied succession of events.

THE UNFOLDING STORY

As Christians, we have the resources to be immune to this. However, popular American churches have ignored the basic practices and principles gifted to us by the ancient church. Our only recourse against this philosophy of sheer change has been to patch together Bible verses from different portions of Scripture in hopes of forming a fixed identity, or a "biblical worldview." We simply cannot build God's house on that kind of sinking sand, regardless of the amount of prooftexts we use to erect it.

I say this directly because I am trying to combat the pat Sunday school answers that stop us from thinking. We imagine that we've solved the problem by claiming "my identity is found in God" or "my identity is found in Scripture." And so, we revert to our individualistic practices or private devotion. This is mistaken. However, if pulling identity-affirming memory verses from disparate parts of the Bible won't stop the anxieties that accompany a world of sheer change, then what will?

With a world as dismembered as ours, how might we put it back together again? I suggest that the first movement toward the solution involves leaning into community. As we discussed in the previous chapter, just as we can't know ourselves all by ourselves, neither can we know God all by ourselves. Christianity is a *received* faith. I don't get to determine what it is according to my understanding of God or Scripture. Therefore, yes, we do get our identity from God. But that only happens when we go back to the first principles of recovering how the early Christian communities came to understand who and what God is. Yes, Scripture is crucial for knowing our identity. However, in the early Christian imagination it was read as an unfolding story of God with his creatures.

The triune God and story are key. To make our way out of Heraclitus's world of flux, Christians must recognize that:

1. Father, Son, and Holy Spirit is the ground, logic, structure, and meaning of all things, holding the world and our identities in coherent existence through time.
2. The biblical story is:
   a. The bedrock of *history*.
   b. Essential to our *communal* identity.
   c. The bedrock of *personal* identity.

The Bible is ultimately a story. A very true story. *There is a narrative character to the Bible as whole, and the plot of the story it tells is the ground of all existence, the truth of all that is, and the meaning of all things.*

THE BEGINNING, END, AND PLOT OF OUR STORIES

Story is the glue that holds communal and personal identity intact. I am now in my thirties, but when I see a picture of my mom carrying me when I was only six months old, I could point to that picture and rightly say, "That's *me* at six months old." Heraclitus would object, arguing that the differences between me at six months old and now are so vast that there's no meaningful way for me to identify the baby in the picture as the same present "me." If we abandon story as a basic way that we make of our lives, Heraclitus can be judged as right. But when our identities are understood through the lens of narrative, I can recognize that the "me" is held together by the unfolding story that constitutes my life. I undergo many stages of change in a lifetime that spans childhood to adulthood—changes like size, strength, knowledge, wisdom, character, and skills, among other things. I take responsibility for my past actions and live each new day as the same "I" of yesterday, building off the knowledge and skills I've been growing and developing. Just so, from my birth onward, my life takes the form of an unfolding story.

Story underpins every human life, and every human life has a beginning and an end that it is tending toward. This story comes from beyond me. I didn't give birth to myself, and the end or fulfillment I am aiming for is one that I cannot bring by my own strength. Just as my birth was dependent on others, so too is my fulfillment. Because we are finite creatures, this is true of everyone. We all exist in a network of relational dependence. I depended on the prior relationship of my parents to bring me here. While here, I depend on my relationship to other people to know who I am. I also depend on a proper relationship to the inanimate world around me: oxygen, water, gravity, etc. All these things and people that I need for my existence are also dependent and finite. What then grounds the shifting, growing, changing, and dependent identities of all finite creatures?

We are back to story. Just as my story comes from beyond me, the story of all creatures comes from beyond us. Put differently, our stories must be fitted to the Alpha and Omega of history. For the Christian, God is the beginning and end of all that is. The plot of our story, then, is only meaningful as we live with the grain of the plot given by the Logos—or in English, the Word. The Word is the truth, order, and ground of all that is. The plot of all history and finite creatures is found in the life, death, and resurrection of Jesus of Nazareth.

THE STORY OF GOD *WITH* US

Scripture consists of story. Despite there being many literary genres in it, without understanding the story, I am left with disjointed "teachings" that I try to clumsily (and often, incoherently) patch together to deal with whatever problem is presenting itself to me right now. Scripture, when faithfully engaged, not only consists of story but is *the* story of all that is. It's a story of Father, Son, and Holy Spirit with creation. The plot and fulfillment of all creation has already been given by the triune God as seen in the life of Jesus. Even if I want to read epistles from Paul or James currently thought by many to be strictly good for teaching, I can't understand what these teachers are doing without understanding their stories considering *the* biblical story.

This is not a new teaching of my own making. This understanding of Scripture was prevalent in the ancient church. One of many examples is Irenaeus of Lyons, a second-century bishop and church father. His importance to Christian thought in its infancy cannot be overstated. One contribution is that he provides the very first extant and explicit teaching on how the church should read her Scriptures. In the second century, the unity of a very young church was being threatened by groups—sometimes called "gnostics"—who engaged Scripture apart from Christian practice. Ironically, these teachers attracted people away from the church by utilizing her texts, and they impressed many lay Christians with how they seemingly read Scripture with deep wisdom. These "gnostics" looked at Scripture as a collection of sayings, stories, and commands from which a reader can extract insights if only they had the right techniques or special knowledge. These techniques looked *back* to Scripture, aiming to make a connection to the text for revelation.

For the church, Scripture is not merely a mine full of discrete opportunities to gain nuggets of insights, if only we knew the proper techniques and channels to acquire them. Irenaeus says that for the church, Scripture is to be read as a unified whole. What makes Scripture a whole is indeed that it tells one single story. For that story to be grasped as a whole, says Irenaeus, the prior knowledge needed is not the techniques of the gnostics. Rather, what needs to be previously known is the story's plot and its main characters. The church—guided by its worship, catechism, teaching, and practice—does in fact know the Bible's main characters. It is our "rule of faith" known within a worshiping community that gives us this prior knowledge (more on this in later chapters) to read Scripture faithfully. When we engage Scripture as Christians within a worshiping community, we recognize the unity of the Bible because:

- it is the same triune God who speaks and acts throughout both Old and New Testaments;
- we live in continuity with, and simply *are* the same community God addresses in Scripture; and
- it is the same cosmic history in which God is still active, speaking, and at work.

When I read Scripture then, I hope to do it first and foremost as a Christian. As such I read it as a worshiper of the triune God, and I recognize the community and the story of which I am a part. This community does not begin and end with my immediate family, my local church context, or people alive in the twentieth and twenty-first centuries, etc. Rather, my story is just as intertwined with my family and my local church as it is with Abraham, Isaac, and Jacob, Moses, Joshua, Deborah, Hannah, Samuel, David, Mary, John, Peter, and Paul. I am also intertwined with the community that was formed around and by this same story—a community called the universal and apostolic Christian church. Early Christians taught me to read this narrative looking for Jesus at every turn, as Jesus himself taught that Moses wrote about him, and all of Scripture is fulfilled in him. It is not the book itself that gives eternal life, says Jesus to the Pharisees, but Scripture is a living word just insofar as the story culminates in the one who is the Way, the Truth, and the Life (John 5:39–47). The triune God-with-us revealed in Christ-with-us is what this identity-making story is about.

Therefore, Scripture is the story of God, but not merely God. Quite shockingly, the triune God's story as told by Scripture is not told without creatures. I will say more about this later. For now, I will simply prefigure what I am going to unpack: Scripture does not begin with myths about a supreme god among other gods, living and fighting in the heavens, earning his right to be God "before" creating a history. In Genesis, we don't get a peek "above" or "behind" history to give us access to what's "really" going on in our world. Rather, Scripture begins with God who is without rival, who merely speaks and so creates history without opposition. He simply gives creation permission to be by speaking to it. We come to know this, then, not through myths of his acts in heaven, but as he relationally engages with what he creates. Hence, creation is mentioned in the very first sentence of Scripture, "In the beginning God *created* . . ." And so, we will move on in the following chapters to tell the story that Scripture narrates of God with his creatures. It's the story of a talkative God who creates history by his word. He not only creates history but is active in it. He introduces himself to creatures, revealing his essence and personal name as he moves the story forward toward its end in him. This is the God and the story in which all of creation lives, and moves, and has its being.

Conclusion

I have spent some time here talking about the necessity of story itself for knowing who we are beyond sheer change. Later, beginning in chapter 4, I will tell the story that the Bible narrates in more detail. For the next chapter, I begin where the story begins: God. Reflection on who God is, as I have already mentioned, has been taken for granted in popular Christian circles. We've opted to do theology without much reflection on God while instead moving right into debates about salvation. An individual reflecting on how God saves apart from community and without reflecting on his triune and essential nature is in error. Much of this book will be aimed at remedying that tragic mistake.

That said, the very beginning of Scripture first makes mention of "God" followed by "created the heavens and the earth." The next chapter will proceed in three connected movements. Because the unity of the Bible is understood as the story of an eternal God relating to finite creatures, and because God reveals his essence in a crucial part of the story when he introduces himself to Moses:

1. Some brief introductory and explicit thoughts need to be shared regarding who God is.
2. This ought to be followed by accounting for how this God relates to creatures.
3. Once an introductory account of the God-creature relationship is given throughout the rest of the following chapter, I will move toward telling the story of Scripture as the triune God-with-us, first in the Old Testament, followed by the New.

If the Christian triune God is the God of the story that keeps the anxious and maddening flux of Heraclitus away, some thoughts on who this God is are warranted. So, who or what is God, and how does he relate to creatures? We will now turn our attention to these questions.

CHAPTER 3

Speaking of God

Divine freedom, like human freedom, is achieved in communion. Freedom is freedom-toward another. Since the exercise of freedom requires a plurality of persons, God's freedom cannot be located in solitariness. The Spirit is the freedom of God permeating, animating, quickening, incorporating, affiliating, engrafting, consummating the creature out of love.

—Catherine Mowry LaCugna

Before picking up right where we left off, here's a quick reminder of some key themes we've been discussing. First, no human being knows themselves all by themselves. We know ourselves in relationship to others, especially those with whom we form intentional community. For the Christian, not only can I not know myself without others, but something in my knowing of God goes drastically missing without community; I know God through the life, teaching, and writing of others. Finally, a community has a meaningful and unified life when it lives within a grander narrative. Story, then, is essential to communal life and self-understanding. Story is what grounds me through the chaotic change of life, and Scripture tells *the* story as it narrates the life of the God of all things, and the life he lives with his creatures. We start this chapter, then, by talking about God as we unpack how he relates to his creatures.

From the outset, the story of the Bible reveals God to be a talkative God. He speaks creation itself into being and introduces himself to those very creatures by speaking to them. He speaks to Adam, Eve, Abraham, and their descendants. God's verbal address to his creatures continues throughout the whole story. He speaks and expects a response. To converse with God is basic to what it means to be a human. We call it prayer.

One prime example of God conversing with a creature is found when Moses responds to God's address. God calls Moses to free his people from the snares of an overwhelmingly powerful kingdom of Egypt. Moses asks, "If I come to the Israelites and say to them 'The God of your ancestors has sent me to you,' and they ask me, 'What is his name?' what shall I say to them?" (Exod 3:13). Essentially, Moses wants to know just who this God is that's speaking to him, and who is promising to free a people. It is interesting that Moses doesn't, as we would, bypass that question and simply rejoice in their promised salvation from Egypt. This is a key portion of the Old Testament narrative. Unsurprisingly, God's answer has been the object of much meditation for Christians throughout history, as it reveals a lot about who God is, and creates inroads to understand how he relates to creatures.

God answers Moses's "who are you" question by giving him three key aspects of his identity. I will briefly discuss each of these aspects in the order God gives them to Moses. God tells Moses:

1. *What* he is: I AM who I AM/I will be who I will be (3:14).

2. His personal name: Yahweh "LORD" (3:15a).

3. His storied identity in history by recalling his relationship to Moses' ancestors: Abraham, Isaac, and Jacob (3:15b).

WHAT GOD IS: I AM

First, God reveals *what* he is. God's answer to Moses's question here is rather puzzling, and it can be translated as both: " I AM who I AM," or "I will be who I will be." Remember when I mentioned that we tend to take the word "God" for granted in modern church-talk? In what follows we will try to remedy this by taking the time to wrestle a bit with God's identity by engaging in what he is. This is, properly speaking, what theology is—the study of God. It's a fruitful and more-than-worthwhile pursuit for the Christian who centers her or his life around this God. Early and medieval Christian theologians have gifted us with some profound ways to grapple with God's identity, and I will be presenting some of those musings in my own words.

God says I AM. What I love about God's response is that it is meant to be revealing, but his revelation confounds his hearers. It's as if in answering Moses's inquiry about who he is, God first wants to demonstrate that he is wholly unlike anything Moses has ever encountered. He's not another god alongside other gods. He's not even the most powerful god. He's not another person in a world of persons. He's not even the most powerful person. He's not another being in a creation full of beings. He's not even the most powerful being. God is basically telling us, "Listen, I know that for humans there is wisdom in thinking in categories, but there are no categories for who I AM. Nor will there ever be. I just AM, and I will be who I will be." This is true only of God. God simply is. Ancient and medieval theology basically puts it this way: God is the "Infinite Act of Existence." He is not *an* existent in the inventory of all things that exist. God is existence itself.

This is a bit much to wrap our heads around, so I will continue by teaching this in different ways. Let me begin by using myself as an example and contrast my human essence with God's essence. *What* I am is easy to discover. All you need to do is look at me. This is part of what's called empirical observation. By looking at me, you can see that I am simply a human among other humans. You can categorize me as a human. What's my basic essence? A human being. We can discover the essences of things in our world in the same way. I can look at the trees on the family farm (as I am currently doing) and point to one and say: "That's a tree among other trees." Why? Because I know what a tree is by knowing its category among the many other things that make up the world. Knowing the category of something in the world is basically the same as knowing its essence. Therefore, according to how these words are used today, essence = a particular thing (tree) in a category (trees). So, if you ask what my essence is, you're asking to which category I belong. Am I an automobile? Well, no. By looking at me, and by what constitutes me, and how I engage the world and the world engages me, I am not a car. My essence, then, is not an automobile, but a human.

Here's where the chasm between God and everything else in the world is really exposed. Two deeply true things about me are: (1) I exist, and (2) my essence is that of a human. So, I am composed as an existent with an essence. God exists, but what exactly is his category or essence? Is his category "god" but only the most powerful one? No! says classical Christian thought. Even if we were to discover that Zeus and his colleagues indeed do exist, God would not be numbered among them and it's not merely because he is more powerful than they. God would not even be in the same category. If humans exist, if trees exist, if gods exist, all have an essence attached to their existence. However, God does not have a category or essence in that way. God is his own "category." What then is God's essence if he doesn't belong to a category? Answer: God's essence is simply that he is (I AM); before Abraham was, he is. God infinitely and necessarily is existence itself. We, as creatures, finitely and dependently exist as beings among other beings. God is not a being among beings. God is—as Paul tells the philosophers of Athens—the one *"in* whom we live and move and have our being." In other words, God is the one in whom all our existences depend. *God's essence is existence itself.* And everything in heaven and on earth that exists has a distinct essence that utterly depends on God for their existence. If there is no God, there is no existence for finite creatures to participate in. God's life creates room for us to live. No God, no existence for anyone. No God, no life for anyone.

I will make one final attempt to explain this as clearly as I know how, by pointing at some concrete examples. Far too often, I hear well-meaning Christians who so deeply want to be pious and faithful to God say things that are mistaken. If God is who classical historical Christian thought says he is, then we would be better served in our modern churches if we ditched these cliches. Think of an example of a leader trying to give others advice for organizing their busy lives. They often do so by proposing a priority list of some kind. The list consists of some variation of the following: God first, family second, work/ministry/church third . . . and so on. If God is indeed I AM, and not a being among beings, or a person or thing alongside other persons or things, then categorizing him as one person/item among others to be categorized is a bad mistake. God is not another person/thing in my life—not even when I insist that he's the most important person/thing in my life. God is triune, and so he simply *is* my life. God *is*.

The next well-meaning thing that is often said by Christians—and this one I admit bothers me more than the first because it makes us say things I find especially awful—is: "I love God more than _____." Usually, it is said from the pulpit from a speaker trying to make it clear that they *really* love Jesus above all else. Most often, the spouse and their children are placed in the blank of that sentence above to show the speaker's serious fidelity. However, loving my neighbor well, much less my wife and child, does not come at the cost of my love for God.[1] This is not a zero-sum game

---

1. Luke 14:26 might be raised as an objection. However, this illustrates yet another problem of the "prooftexting" of Bible verses that I will address in more detail throughout this book. For now, I will simply note two things. First, there are obvious exegetical difficulties of squaring a "plain reading" of Luke 14:26 with commands for children to honor their fathers and mothers (Exod 20:12), for husbands to love their wives as Christ loves the church (Eph 5:25; cf. 1 Pet 3:1–7), and the sheer impossibility of claiming to love God who we do not see when we cannot love a brother or sister who we do see (1 John 4:20–21). There are many more biblical texts that could be noted. Second, this text is addressing a people for whom following Christ meant following something radically new, which meant a decisive break from their long-standing familial and religious traditions in which their identities had been previously formed. That does not quite square with me hating my wife and son in a household whose aim is to be conformed to the image and likeness of Christ. Having said that, what I find interesting is that later when Paul is addressing men or women who are married to unbelieving spouses, for the sake of their households, Paul encourages them to remain with them and thus sanctify their

whereby to love someone well is a threat to taking away love that should be allocated for God. There is no true love "outside" of God.

God *is* Love (1 John 4:8). That is not the same as claiming that God is a being who *has* the most love, or even is the most loving. God doesn't have an essence to which love belongs. God simply is Love. Or, to put in classical language, God is the Infinite Act of Existence that is the eternal Love shared between Father, Son, and Spirit. The difference between being Love itself and having the most love is absolute. A being who is most loving is merely a being who is set alongside other loving beings. If these beings, or people, or things, or gods, were to compete with one another as to which one was the most loving, the being called "God" would win. But Christians don't claim that God is most loving. We claim that God is Love. This means that what enables anything to have love at all is that it is wholly and utterly dependent on the Love that God is. If there is no God who is infinite Love, there would be no finite love in existence to be shared between people. Finite love exists because it borrows from the Love that God is. Therefore, in response to saying, "I love God more than my wife and kids," I want to insist that my love for God is not in competition with my love for my family. Rather, God's life is the pure Love that I am utterly dependent upon to love my family faithfully.

Finally, I will tie a bow on this by naming other predicates. God is not a God who is true, nor is he a true thing alongside other true things in the world. God is the Truth that makes it possible for true things to exist. True things borrow their trueness from God. God is not a life among other lives. God is *the* Life in which all other lives depend on to live. One more time, God is not an existent, or a thing that exists. God is the Infinite Act of Existence. God is existence itself, and all other things that exist fully depend on him at every moment for their existence. God doesn't exist merely *in* reality, God is the reality in which all other things live, move, and have their being. In revealing *what* he is to Moses, we simply find out *that* he is. In the language of philosophical theology: *that*

---

spouses and their children (1 Cor 7:10–16). Theologically speaking, more can be said, but this will suffice for now.

PART I | (RE)INTERPRETING THE WORLD

God is, is the same as *what* God is. Or better, God's existence (that he is) is exactly the same as his essence (what he is). God is. Or, to put it in biblical language by quoting God to Moses and Jesus to the Pharisees: "I AM."

THE ACTIVE GOD WHO SPEAKS

In this section, I will combine items two and three in God's spoken revelation to Moses of who he is. After revealing to Moses *what* he is, he tells Moses his personal name, Yahweh, and connects the name to his story with Moses's ancestors, Abraham, Isaac, and Jacob.

God reveals his personal name to Moses. Let's first look at personal names from our creaturely point of view. This ought to be a little easier to wrap our minds around considering that personal names are used in our shared experience. Understanding how they function for us can help us analogously understand how they function when God introduces himself to us. Personal names are necessary for our identity. As beings-in-relation, our names only carry meaning according to how we relate to the world around us. For example, my name is Ray. There are many Rays in the world, (even some with the same last name) and if you want to tell others about which Ray you're talking about, you will need to point to how I act and relate in the world. "Do you know Ray Robles? He's the one who_____."

There are many ways one could fill in this blank: He's the one who . . . is Christina's husband, is Marlon's dad, teaches and writes theology, practices Brazilian Jiu Jitsu, etc. The overall network of my first and last name connected to my actions and relationships tell you *who* I am, and so gives my name its meaning and distinguishes me from everyone else. My name is how you address me, and *who* I am is mostly known by having a direct history with me or by knowing of my life's relationships and actions. Therefore, I am Ray Robles, the tolerable Christian, son/husband/father/friend/colleague of_____, who_____.

The Old Testament narratively reveals God to be two things at once. First, as we just talked about in the previous section, he is the Lord and author of the biblical story, transcending it as the Infinite Act of Existence. Second, not only does he transcend the story, he also acts as a character within it. When working from within the narrative, God speaks to people and does acts among them. He relates to people in history, and so we get to know him by these acts. When God gives his personal name of Yahweh to Moses, he connects it to his conversations and acts within the history. Put differently, he connects his name with the life he lived among Moses's ancestors. Moses knows the story of his people as their story with their God, who has now revealed his name. Not only is he the God of the storied past, he is also the God who is the present mover of history. He will come to be better known by Moses and his people as he continues to live his story with them. They will come to know God as the one who: talked to Moses through the burning bush, sent Moses to Pharaoh, sent plagues to Egypt, freed Israel from slavery. Just prior to liberating Israel, God reveals himself. He does this by not only recounting his past acts with their forefathers and by living and acting within their present, but also by opening their lives up to new possibilities through a promised future. Yahweh is a God who makes promises and so binds their future to his.

> Say therefore to the Israelites, "I am the Lord, and I will free you from the burdens of the Egyptians and deliver you from slavery to them. I will redeem you with an outstretched arm and with mighty acts of judgment. I will take you as my people, and I will be your God. You shall know that I am the Lord your God, who has freed you from the burdens of the Egyptians. I will bring you into the land that I swore to give to Abraham, Isaac, and Jacob; I will give it to you for a possession. I am the Lord." (Exod 6:6–8)

As the story unfolds, Yahweh makes good on his spoken promises. He delivers them from the hand of Pharaoh. Once they are delivered, God speaks to Moses yet again on the other side of the

Red Sea, revealing to him what it will look like for Israel to be a freed people oriented toward Yahweh as their God. At this point in the narrative, the Israelites have only known four hundred years of slavery. Their identities are that of slaves. The Ten Commandments are there to teach a people who have only known slavery what it looks like to live like a community of God's people. Again, righteousness is living by faith, which looks like relating rightly with God as we relate rightly with one another.

Freed people live in step with the God who frees them, not with those gods who enslaved them: "You shall have no other gods before me." God's aim is not merely God-ward living at the cost of one another. Rather, in being freed to rightly love God—who acts in history, makes promises, and brings freedom—we learn what it looks like to live with one another as a free community. Communities freed by God to live for God don't kill, steal, or covet because it violates the righteousness of the community. If I can't live in right standing with my neighbor or community, I cannot live in right standing with God. A refusal to righteously belong to his community is a refusal to righteously belong to God. A truly freed community lives righteously with each other, and that righteous living *with* each other is simultaneously righteous living *with* God. I hammer this point so thoroughly because our imaginations are not geared to see it. We're far too comfortable with an aloof God who resides safely "up there" and merely "looks down at us" and intermittently "intervenes" when he is so compelled. Such a God is distant from us and uninvolved with us. Other than his "interventions"—whether sovereign or compelled—he remains removed and unsullied by history. As I will continue to insist throughout this work, that is not the God of the gospel.

The God of the gospel is involved and talkative at every turn. His story with us, culminating in his incarnation, is nothing less than his identification with us. God refuses to have his story told without us. What we do to each other, we do to him. So, Jesus says:

> "'You shall love the Lord your God with all your heart, and with all your soul, and with all your mind.' This is the greatest and first commandment. And a second is like

it: "You shall love your neighbor as yourself." On these two commandments hang all the law and the prophets.'" (Matt 22:37–40)

I want readers to notice how Jesus has no issues identifying himself with creatures in history to the point where the second command to love our neighbors "is like" the first. As Scripture witnesses to again and again, to love your neighbor is to love God. This is true, whether we are noticing how God speaks in, through, and with his creatures in the Old Testament, or in the teachings of Jesus himself (Matt 22:39; Mark 12:29–31, Luke 10:27). Loving God and loving neighbor as yourself are simply two movements of the same act. This is a consistent and ever-present theme in the biblical narrative.

When Paul and James use the same language of summing up all the law in the prophets, they don't even mention loving God. It is as though Paul and James have been so shaped by God-with-us, that they assume that loving your neighbor well simply is honoring, obeying, and loving God (Rom 13:8–10; Gal 5:14; Jas 2:8). This can be true of God and creatures because God is not a being among beings, or a creature among creatures. The love I love my neighbor well with is nothing less than a finite expression of the Love that God *is*. I need not turn my back on my neighbor or my family to love God. There is no zero-sum game. God is the Infinite Act of Existence in whom we live and move and have our being; yet he lives his story with us, he talks to us, moves in us, dwells in and with us. Indeed, God is closer to us than we are to ourselves.

Conclusion

Before we develop these themes further throughout the rest of the book, and before we move on to telling our identity-giving story in the next chapter, here is a brief outline of what I have said about who God is so far:

- God creates by speaking and acting in history.

- God acts among and speaks to creatures. He reminds them of his works in their past while simultaneously binding himself to them through a promised future.
- God is who he is and cannot be categorized alongside other things in heaven or on earth.
- God reveals his name and identifies himself by his acts in history.
- God is not averse to identifying himself with creatures. To love God well is to love others well.

Now that we have established these key themes that I will develop throughout the book, what will begin to emerge is how God unifies himself with his creatures in the biblical story. I've said very little about the doctrine of the Trinity so far, but it will feature more prominently as this book develops. For now, we remind you that while he transcends the story because he is the author and mover of it, he's also ever present and active throughout the story of Scripture. He is not a distanced God up in the sky looking down at us but is known by his actions in and with us.

We are, then, *not* in a meaningless Heraclitian flux. Amidst the chaos and change there is a story of a talkative God, I AM, in whom we live and move and have our being. He has always been at work among a people, moving their story forward as he holds them in existence. The same God is still speaking, and that God is still making promises. He has a name, and his story is one in which he is ever-present and at work, even within the valleys of our finite lives. He began a good story, and the *fullness* of the goodness and glory of that story is yet to be revealed. That is a story we have lost touch with as Christians. Allow me to tell you the beginning of that true and identity-orienting story in the next chapter.

CHAPTER 4

The God Who Moves History

The Holy Spirit was at our side from the very beginning, in every one of God's plans for us, foretelling the future, showing forth the present, and recalling the past.

—Irenaeus

Since this Spirit is infinitely wise and loving, if He takes possession of a shepherd, he makes him a Psalmist, subduing evil spirits by his song and proclaims him King of Israel; if He takes a goatherd and scraper of sycamore fruit, He makes him a Prophet.

—Gregory Nazianzen

In the following two chapters, I am going to offer a reading of both Old and New Testaments. I have demonstrated that for the early Christians, what makes Scripture a whole, unified, and coherent text is that while it contains many stories, it ultimately tells one single overarching story. Throughout both testaments, it is the story of the same triune God both creating and animating history while also acting within it. This talkative God is especially active in and among his people. As I further suggested in the previous chapter, those of us who are in him today, live in continuity with—and simply *are*—the same community God addresses in Scripture. Therefore, in contrast to the storyless, fragmented, fluctuating, and merely reactive existence of those who live in a world of sheer change, our identities are undergirded by the ancient story of God-with-us.

In this chapter, we will take a brief bird's-eye view of the first act of the overarching story of Scripture—the Old Testament. For the purposes of this book, I want to emphasize something that is often glossed over when considering the biblical narrative. I will be telling the story of the Old Testament while paying close attention to the work of the Holy Spirit. This emphasis will help us better grasp the God-world relationship as I have been presenting it so far in this book and will continue to do throughout. It will also help further highlight what I hope to unpack in the next chapter: the significance of the kingdom of God in the New Testament and its significance for the future-oriented mission of the people of God.

THE GIVER OF LIFE WHO SPEAKS THROUGH THE PROPHETS

Regarding the Holy Spirit, ancient Christian creeds assert that we believe "in the Holy Spirit, the Lord, *the giver of life* . . . who has *spoken through the prophets*." It is no wonder the ancient church discerned these as key characteristics of the Holy Spirit as these are dominant themes of the Spirit's ministry throughout the Christian Scriptures. Thus, Christian dogma about the Holy Spirit connects the Spirit of God to:

- Life itself.
- Prophetic speech and action.

In the Old Testament, the Spirit of God is often referred to as the *ruach* of God (used around 378 times), which means the very wind and breath of God. The breath of God is the very principle of life. In the Old Testament, creaturely life can be understood as derived from the all-inhering Spirit of Yahweh. God's Spirit creates life (Gen 1; Job 33:4) and *is* life itself (Ps 104:29–30). This Spirit of God, then, creates and animates all creatures so that there is no such thing as Spirit-less creation. No Spirit in creation means no creation at all. Therefore, the Holy Spirit is the opposite of death; he is basic to life itself.

Not only does the Old Testament talk about God's Spirit as life itself, but by that same life-giving Spirit, God creatively transforms *history*, drawing it toward what God intends. "The Spirit-Breath is first and foremost what causes humanity to act so that God's plan in history may be fulfilled."[1] Therefore, the Holy Spirit is the opposite of hopelessness; he's the principle of history's hope-filled fulfillment.

Early Christians discerned that history itself is moved and lurched forward as the Spirit of God empowers the Bible's charismatic leaders to *act* and *speak* prophetically. We see this in the lives of Moses, the judges, the early kings, and the prophets. Before God's people had kings and classic prophets, God's Spirit empowered Moses who, as some Old Testament scholars have noted, is the quintessential prophet and exemplar for Israel's forthcoming prophets.[2] Indeed Scripture itself also affirms, "Never since has there arisen a prophet in Israel like Moses, whom the Lord knew face to face" (Deut 34:10). It is through Moses, and the charismatic leaders after him, that God creates a people in history and moves history itself toward fulfillment. The Spirit comes upon these and other preexilic leaders of Israel to inspire the kind of prophecy that confronts the kings of world and throws down the hopeless status quo for the sake of moving history toward what God intends. For some examples:

- The immediate result of God dispersing "some of the spirit" that is on Moses to the seventy elders is that they became leaders who prophesied (Num 11:17–30).
- When it comes to the judges, God's creative Spirit calls each one into their roles of leadership, and their historically

---

1. Congar, *I Believe in the Holy Spirit*, 4.
2. Among many others, Moore, *Spirit of the Old Testament*, 71.

PART I | (RE)INTERPRETING THE WORLD

significant actions explicitly involve the Spirit of God (Judg 3:10; 6:34; 11:29; 13:25).[3]

- The same happens with Saul, the first king of Israel (1 Sam 10:10–11; 11:6–7).
- David, the king *par excellence*, experiences the Spirit of Yahweh coming mightily upon him to take over the role of king and to speak as a prophet (1 Sam 16:13). Moreover, as a prophet, David claims himself as one to speak promises *for* God (2 Sam 23:1–7).

Surprisingly, prophesying was not reserved for those called prophets or kings but could also emerge from anyone upon whom the Spirit of God rested (1 Sam 10:10–11; 19:20ff; 1 Chr 12:18). In Numbers 22:41—24:25, we get a shocking account of God's Spirit-inspired prophetic activity. When the Spirit of God comes upon a corrupt diviner named Balaam who was hired to curse Israel, despite himself, Balaam speaks true promises rather than false curses precisely because "the Spirit of God came upon him" (Num 24:2). Therefore, according to both the early church and the Old Testament biblical witness, the Holy Spirit is the giver of life and speaks through the prophets to move history toward its fulfillment.

THE SPIRIT OF THE PROMISE

Whatever distinctions one wants to make between the preexilic prophesying just described and that of the later classic prophets, when the Holy Spirit comes upon someone, they are granted the ability to speak on God's behalf. I also noted that it is not unheard of for the Spirit to come upon those we would least expect. Israel's story begins as the God of all creation picks a particular and unimpressive people to live his own history alongside them—Abraham and Sarah. God joins himself to them by speaking to them. From the outset, his word to them is a promise. God could have given

---

3. For a more exhaustive treatment on this subject in particular, see Martin, *Unheard Voice of God*.

this promise to a powerful king. But instead, through this old man and barren woman, God will create a vast nation that will bless all nations (Gen 12:1–3).

When the offspring of Abraham and Sarah come to be known as Israel, after being led through much turbulence under charismatic leaders, prophets, and judges, they request for God to grant them a king so that they can reflect the kingdoms around them. Therefore, the kingdom of Israel came to be set alongside others because they asked for a king to govern them "like other nations" (1 Sam 8:5). In this ancient context, the power of a kingdom was a direct reflection of the supremacy of their god or gods. If a kingdom was the most powerful it proved their god(s) to be the true and most powerful god(s).

Israel's kingdom was marked by a series of successes and failures due to their faithfulness or lack thereof. A key moment for the kingdom of Israel was the building of the first temple under the leadership of King Solomon. The temple was a fixed display that the presence of God was with them in the land he had promised Abraham. Given the context, the overthrow of God's people, the destruction of the temple, and their being scattered and exiled was emphatically significant. In their defeat and exile, had Yahweh been disproven as supreme? A conquered people correlate to a conquered god, therefore it would seem that Yahweh was unfit to be Lord of all.

However, when the life-giving and history-creating Spirit of God came upon the prophets of Yahweh, they told a different and religiously unprecedented story. Their God, Yahweh, was the very one responsible for their exile, due to Israel's lack of faithfulness. They lived unrighteously before God as they succumbed to the idols of the surrounding nations. They also lived unjustly with one another and with those around them, failing in their vocation to be a blessing to others—also in this way, they were unrighteous. Failing to live righteously with God and with each other meant they were alienated from God, from each other, and from other nations.

God could overthrow his own people without ceasing to be supreme because Yahweh was without rival. He wasn't insecure about his standing against the so-called gods of other nations. This left God's people with a pressing question: Where is the fulfillment of the promised blessing to Abraham? Is Yahweh still their God and is Israel still God's people? Can they still have hope for justice and peace now that they face possible extinction without a fixed identity?

As the story unfolds, we learn that judgment does not ultimately thwart the promises of God but moves toward them. According to the prophets, judgment and exile do not mark the end of God's covenant. God still binds himself to the promises he makes to his people despite their unfaithfulness. Therefore, there is another side to the message of the prophets. That other side of the prophetic message of judgment is that God will make good on his promises, so he will restore Israel and their mission to bless other nations.

THE SPIRIT OF HOPE

Isaiah and Ezekiel (among others), by the power of the Holy Spirit, speak prophetically to Israel under threat of extinction. The book of Ezekiel begins with the dynamic wind of God (1:4, 17, 20–21) later revealed to be God's life-giving Spirit that inspires an eschatological, or future-worldly, vision of hope where God overcomes Israel's alienation from himself (39:29). In chapter 37, this beyond-hopeless situation is illustrated by a valley of dry bones. Their alienation from God and the death it has wrought is to be overcome by God's promise to give his Spirit for the sake of resurrecting a seemingly beyond dead people.

For Ezekiel, as in the rest of the Old Testament, the Spirit is life itself. True to his character in the biblical narrative, the Spirit of God inspires prophecy to bring life and eschatological hope where death and sheer hopelessness have seemed to have won the day. Here, "Ezekiel is brought to the valley plain (cf. 3:11; 8:4), which had been a place where judgment had to be suffered, but now becomes the place where God triumphs over death and serves as an impressive symbol of God's resurrecting power." This text demonstrates once again that "spirit transportation in Ezekiel (cf. 3:12, 14, 8:3; 40:1), which is always induced by the 'hand of God,' is an expression often used to describe God's possession, inspiration, and empowering of the prophet."[4] The Spirit who inspires prophetic speech and action in Ezekiel is also two things at once for God's people who are seemingly beyond dead (as the valley of dry bones suggests):

- The Holy Spirit is the object of Israel's hope.
- The Holy Spirit is the guarantee as God's people continue to live history with him that he will make good on his otherworldly promises.

Paul will later use the language of "down payment" to also suggest that the Holy Spirit is the guarantee that God will make good on his promises (2 Cor 1:22; 5:5; Eph 1:13–14).

God shows Ezekiel the valley and asks, "Can these bones live?" The history of Israel has now forced this question upon them. Is death the end of us all? Can death be undone? Living in the wake of the failure to have walked in God's promises, Israel has been called to hope again despite their history seeming to have ended up as a heap of dead and dry bones. Who will finally free them from their own unfaithfulness? Who will finally free them from the threat of being ruled by wicked leaders, or leaders who are constantly under threat of exile or enslavement from more powerful armies?

The world's kings have failed to bring righteousness, so what comes next will have to be an act of God himself ruling as king. The expectations from the mouth of the prophets were for a prophet and king who will do the will of God perfectly (as the kings and prophets had failed to do) and so usher in the kingdom that God has been working to establish. They now hoped for a Christ, an Anointed One to do just this. The prophets declare that God's people *will* triumph because we will be gathered by and around *the* Prophet and King. He will be *the* Spirit-Bearer that will bring not

---

4. Schafroth, "'Spirit' References in Ezekiel 36 and 37," 71–73.

only peace for God's people, but peace for all creation (Isa 11:2–9; 42:1).

This hope will develop to contain a communal aspect. Death will not reign, because in the last days, *all* of God's people will be prophetic bearers of his life-giving Spirit (Joel 2:28). Isaiah agrees as God speaks through him that "my Spirit which is upon you, and my words which I have put in your mouth, shall not depart out of your mouth, or out of the mouth . . . of your children's children . . . from this time forth and forevermore" (Isa 59:21). So, we await the King, the prophetic Spirit-Bearer who will not only bear the Spirit, but freely pour the Spirit out to create a community that will live and speak the Word of the Lord.

Conclusion

Once again, this chapter contained a telling of the Old Testament as the story of the active God-with-us who speaks, makes promises, and acts in history while moving it toward its fulfillment. It emphasized the life and work of the Holy Spirit throughout the narrative as the giver of life who speaks through the prophets. In the following chapter, I will give an account of the story of Jesus, as the Spirit-Bearer, the Promised King who also bears the Promise itself—the life-giving Holy Spirit. Jesus does not hoard the Spirit but gives him for the sake of creating a community of prophets. The outpouring of the Holy Spirit inaugurates new creation, the kingdom of God—the reality toward which creation finds its fulfillment. Thus, in the following chapter, we continue to the tell the story of Scripture by looking at the New Testament as the second act of the ancient story of God-with-us.

CHAPTER 5

The Spirited Testimony of Jesus

Then I fell down at his feet to worship him, but he said to me, "You must not do that! I am a fellow servant with you and your comrades who hold to the testimony of Jesus. Worship God! For the testimony of Jesus is the spirit of prophecy."

—REVELATION 19:10

AS PROMISED, I AM GOING to continue telling the story of the Bible by now taking a close look at the New Testament. Before diving in, I must briefly put on the brakes and take the time to unpack a crucial teaching found throughout its pages: the kingdom of God. I believe understanding this concept will prove fruitful to better understand the story of the New Testament. What, then, is the kingdom of God?

According to Jesus, the kingdom of God is central to his life and teaching. He told the crowds who were awestruck by his signs, "I must proclaim the good news of the kingdom of God to other cities also; for I was sent for this purpose" (Luke 4:43). He will go on to spell out the strangeness of his message by giving a host of parables that people struggled to understand. We often think that Jesus told parables to make his teachings clearer, but Jesus gives the opposite reason. When talking to the disciples he tells them "To you it has been given to know the secrets of the kingdom of God; but to others I speak in parables, so that 'looking they may not perceive, and listening they may not understand'" (Luke 8:10). Just what then is the good news of the kingdom of God? How—considering its profound strangeness—does it relate to the world as we know it?

THE SPIRIT OF THE KINGDOM

Ancient Jewish traditions understood the world as divided into two distinct periods:

1. *The present age*: This was the age as they were currently experiencing it. The "present age" is an age with evil and death still looming large over creatures and the various spheres within creation like institutions, politics, social relationships, etc. All these realities in the "present age" are subject to decay, illness, scarcity, and finitude along with the fear of death that accompany a reality experienced in this fashion.

2. *The age to come*: Considering that the present age is marred by darkness, the "age to come" is nothing less than the *fullness* of God's kingdom crashing down upon and completely eradicating the death and evil that characterize the present age. The age to come is a world without limit or end. It is a world marked by the healing, reconciliation, and fullness of life so that there is no need to fear scarcity or death. The age to come is none other than the promised kingdom of God that Jesus taught and demonstrated. So here, we get a picture of two radically separate realities that never touch.

Between the problems of the present age that we all experience, and the promise of the age to come, where do the "last days" fit in? The "last days" was a name given to the time in history where the goodness of the "age to come," or the kingdom of God—we can use "age to come" and "kingdom of God" interchangeably—has begun its "overlap" with the present age without completely overcoming it. The future of what God intends for creation (the kingdom of God) has now begun to break into the present age of darkness so that there is now overlap between these two ages. That period of the "overlap," so to speak, is called the "last days." That is, we live in a day where creation is still subjected to decay. People are still getting sick and dying while evil remains prevalent in various forms, which are marks of the present age. However, the last days marks a time where the kingdom of God is more readily available and when it comes upon us, there is healing, deliverance, and freedom. In the last days, these events are signs that when the kingdom of God *fully* arrives at the appearing of Jesus in glory, God will make good on his promise to completely overcome and eradicate the evil of the present age. Until then, the last days is the reality we live in, in which evil is prevalent, but God is currently reigning, and he will do so until all his enemies are put under his feet (see 1 Cor 15).

Here's where the kingdom of God, eschatology, and the Holy Spirit are joined at the hip. Where the Holy Spirit manifests, we see the realities of the future-coming-kingdom crashing into our present as signs that God will make good on his promise. The "last days," then, are not a name for a time span near the end of history. While this pushes against the more popular imagination of contemporary apocalyptic church-talk, the "last days" have nothing to do with "end times." In fact, I would suggest we dispense with "end times" language altogether. It has unnecessarily wrought fear, doomsdayism, escapism, and hopelessness to a people called to live with a God whose Spirit gives life to dry bones.

Indeed, we have been in the last days since the events of Pentecost as Peter explicitly states that the events of Acts 2 are a fulfillment of "What was spoken through the prophet Joel: in the *last days* it will be, God declares, that I will pour out my Spirit on all flesh, and your sons and daughters shall prophesy . . ." (Acts 2:17). The Holy Spirit being poured out on all flesh is the "down payment" that inaugurates the kingdom of God by creating a community of prophets that is the church. It's a community that while it is in the world (and so its people are still subjected to death like everyone else), it is not *of* the world because the Spirit that created it is from the age to come. That is, the Spirit that creates the church is the Spirit of the kingdom of God. The church is a community formed to witness from the perspective of the future-coming kingdom, hence we are a community of prophets.

We are a community of prophets because we prophesy with our voices, with our deeds, and the kinds of church communities we embody, demonstrating that the evils of this present age have an expiration date. This is what it means to be witnesses. Therefore, witnessing is not handing out tracts at a gas station, standing on a boardwalk with picket signs and a bullhorn, or telling your friend at work about Jesus (not that this last one is at all wrong). Jesus connects the power brought by the Holy Spirit to communal witnessing (Acts 1:8). The Holy Spirit is the reality of the age to come, and when he comes upon us, he empowers the people of God to live as a community not of this world, but of the kingdom that God will one day fully consummate when he appears in the fullness of his glory at the end of the ages. This is what it means to be communal witnesses, this is what it means to be a community of prophets. Hence, the church and the kingdom of God cannot be separated.[1]

THE SPIRIT-BEARING KING

Now, let's pick back up where we left off on the story of Scripture. To briefly recap, after the failure of kings and of God's people to live righteously before God and one another, the hope for the creative, life-giving, transforming, age-to-come-bringing, prophecy-inspiring Spirit of Yahweh is now aimed at hoping for a single Spirit-Bearer. Frustrated by the problems wrought by human kings, the people of God now await one whose action in the world will be identical with the action of God. We also noted that through this one person, there is a hope that there would emerge from those submitted to this king, a *community* of prophets. That is, a community that lives by the reality of the kingdom of God. There were several sects of Jews who did not give up hope that such

---

1. For a more exhaustive yet accessible treatment on the close relationship between the kingdom of God and the church written by a New Testament scholar, see McKnight, *Kingdom Conspiracy*.

a one was indeed coming. Each sect had different expectations for what that would look like. In a world where these sects were waiting with their own expectations for the kingdom of God to come to earth through the Messiah, a strange grasshopper-eating man who had no voice within the city gates taught, prophesied, and baptized from outside of the city. He was a sign that the kingdom of God was not going to be what anyone expected. So, at the heart of his message, he proclaimed to the Pharisees, Sadducees, Essenes, and Zealots, among others, "Repent, for the kingdom of God is at hand!"

Roger Stronstad, a New Testament scholar who specializes in the writings of Luke, suggests that when one reads Luke-Acts closely, the reader can find "everything which Luke reports Jesus as doing and saying are the works and words of the eschatological anointed prophet" and notes this as a dominant theme present in the text.[2] In the Gospels, the life of Jesus is consistently Spirit-focused as his birth, baptism, and works are again and again, by the power of the Holy Spirit. Even from the very moment of his conception, as Scripture witnesses to and ancient Christians confessed, Jesus was "conceived by the power of the Holy Spirit." John is explicit on this point as well. He insists that Jesus's "birth is not the result of physical, sexual, or human means but comes from God himself (John 1:13). This activity will later be attributed to the work of the Spirit."[3] Jesus was conceived, that is, in a way that no one else in history had been or will be. The life to follow is one that is fully human and fully God. Jesus is not merely *a* human in an identical way that you and I are. Some commentary is here warranted.

We seem to know this in part, but never really parse out the fullness of the implications the way that the earliest Christian thinkers did. Getting into the very depth of who Jesus was in his very being was essential for Christians throughout most of church history. I will discuss more fully in Part II of this book how and why we stopped talking about God—neglecting reflection on the

---

2. Stronstad, *Prophethood of All Believers*, 3.
3. Thomas, *He Loved Them Until the End*, 35.

PART I | (RE)INTERPRETING THE WORLD

Trinity and Christ—and the consequences it has wrought to our speech, acts, and lives as Christians. Because we tend to think that theology revolves *solely* around understanding how God saves individuals, I will here succumb to that temptation to make it easier for the reader to understand this point. We all know that my personal death does nothing for all humanity. It will only impact those closest to me, and perhaps some others who knew me. Other than that, my death will only mean that I am gone and unavailable to those who are living on this side of the veil. Why? Because I am just *a* human born of a human mother and father, and so my death doesn't impact *all* of humanity, much less all of creation. My death doesn't provide anything for all of humanity. However, we don't say this of Jesus. We know Jesus's life, death, and resurrection somehow provides access to something—what we call salvation—to creatures. Why? Because of his *being* as fully God and fully man. There's nothing that happens to Jesus that doesn't also touch humanity. Just so, he is the *Logos* made flesh. Jesus is not merely *a* human being; he is humanity itself. Because he is God, his becoming a creature impacts *all* of creaturely reality. This is a criminally brief treatment for now, but I will come back to this later.

Just as the Spirit of Yahweh creates, transcends, and transforms history by breathing on creation and inspiring prophetic acts that move history and bring life in the Old Testament, the same is true of significant events narrated in the life of Jesus in the New Testament. From the very beginning, as the Spirit hovered over the waters to inaugurate creation in Genesis 1:2, so the Spirit overshadows Mary to bring Jesus, the bearer of new creation. Mary brings forth the child in the same manner that the prophets of old brought forth their words—by the Spirit. In all four Gospels, Jesus's baptism is identified as the Spirit's descent upon Jesus, which inaugurates his public ministry (Matt 3:13–17; Mark 1:9–11; Luke 3:21–22; John 1:29–34). Yet, as all these texts show, Jesus does not hoard the Spirit, or bear him for his own sake. Rather, Jesus bears the Spirit faithfully in order to give him as life-giving gift. "I have baptized you with water," says John the Baptist, "but he will baptize *you with the Holy Spirit*" (Mark 1:7–8 *par*). Everything

Jesus says and does are the words and acts of an eschatological Spirit-bearing and Spirit-giving prophet, and Matthew and Mark testify that Jesus's healing works are specifically done in the Spirit of God (Matt 12:28; Mark 3:29–30). Once again, this power of the Holy Spirit in and through the healing life of Jesus is explicitly identified as the breaking-in of the "kingdom of God" (Matt 12:28; Mark 3:29–30). So, Luke (4:16–30) forms a theology out of these insights, interpreting Isaiah's promise of *the* prophet (Isa 6:1–4) to demonstrate that Jesus is this very one. This is the one who, as the baptismal narratives have already foreshadowed, will give the Spirit that he bears (Luke 11:13).

THE SPIRIT-GIVING KING

Once the biblical narrative moves from Jesus being the Spirit-bearer of the Gospels to the Spirit-giver in Acts, the leaders of the new community of prophets speak prophetically when filled with the Spirit. Acts 4:8 displays a kind of archetype: "Then Peter, filled with the Holy Spirit, *said* . . ." At every turn, the life and words of church's leaders appear just as they did for Jesus, as given by the Spirit (Acts 4:31; 5:32; 6:3, 5, 10; 7:55–56; 13:4; 15:28; 19:21; 20:22–23); by this very Spirit, they heard the "other-worldly" and directional word of God himself (Acts 8:29; 10:19–20; 11:12; 13:2, 4; 16:6–7; 21:4).

This Spirit is the same creative, death-defying Spirit we read about in Ezekiel; the essence of the Spirit is sheer life itself that raised Jesus from dead (Rom 1:4, 8:1–27; 1 Pet 3:18; 4:6). Moreover, this Spirit is, at the same time, the Spirit *of* Jesus and the Spirit *of* prophecy (Acts 17:1). When Christian communities speak prophetically it is none other than the living and risen Jesus who sends his Spirit to create the prophetic speech and acts. So, says John, "the testimony of Jesus is the spirit of prophecy" (Rev 19:10). The very life of Jesus is animated and borne along by the Spirit of prophecy. Jesus gives his Spirit of prophecy to his people, which brings us back to Peter's interpretation of the Acts 2 events: "This Jesus God raised up . . . Being therefore exalted at the right hand of God . . . , he has poured out this which you see and hear" (vv. 32–33). This outpouring inaugurates the kingdom and creates the church; this outpouring creates a community of prophets, which is to say the same thing.

I feel I need to say a bit more here before moving on. I fear that when I talk about the Spirit as gift, readers may misread what I mean and so lose the force of the actual claim I am making. I am not saying that God gives us a gift in the same way we give gifts to each other. Remember, we discussed at length why God is not a being among beings. With that in mind, there are limits to who we are as finite persons that God does not share, and so what it means for him to give us the gift of his Spirit and what it means for us to give gifts to each other cannot simply be equated. In my very being, in my very personhood, I am (modernly speaking) an isolated individual who may choose to relate to other isolated individuals in a benevolent way by giving them something that may add value or enjoyment to their lives. This is what it means for finite beings to give gifts to each other. But once the gift is given, our isolated selves remain as isolated and separated selves until we choose to interact with one another again. I cannot give you a gift that becomes one with you, and my giving you a gift does not quite make us one with each other, either.

Making this shift is crucial to better understand who God is and how he relates to his creation in a way that early Christians did, which we have now lost touch with. This shift is crucial to understanding a litany of biblical texts that we tend to gloss over in our incessant modern quests to read Scripture as a moral code, a framework of individual salvation, or a text of good advice to be immediately applied. I will note how this shift happened in a later chapter, but for now, let's return to Scripture to show how the giving of the Spirit links us, and at-ones us with God and with each other.

CREATING ROOM IN THE LIFE OF GOD

So far, we have talked a lot about the day of Pentecost and the creative significance of the Spirit being given as a gift to transform the people of God into the body of Christ—a community of prophets. There is an important component that is even more astonishing once we break past the familiarities of making such statements in Christian circles. There is, I think, a deeper truth that is often missed. And that is that the ascension of Jesus and the pouring out of his Spirit initiate an intimacy, a nearness, and a depth of relationship between God and his creatures that makes speaking of any kind of separation between God and creatures unthinkable. To remind the reader of what I briefly touched on earlier, classical Christian theology rightly insists that at the very core of *what* God is, we cannot say that God is a being among beings, or a person among persons. God cannot be listed as another item in the inventory of things or beings that make up (constitute) the universe. I can't take inventory of the things around me and list God as one of them. That is, I can't look around and note the things and people that I see and say: it's me, my wife, my son, my job, these trees, those clouds, and God. This, again, is crucial to understanding the doctrine of the Trinity—hence the reason our modern preaching is so lacking on this point that we often think God is a mathematical problem to be solved—which I will also touch on later. But for now, it will suffice to simply give this brief reminder and look at just a small sample of relevant biblical texts. We'll begin by looking at what John 14:1–7 says.

> "Do not let your hearts be troubled. Believe in God, believe also in me. In my Father's house there are many dwelling places. If it were not so, would I have told you that I go to prepare a place for you? And if I go and prepare a place for you, I will come again and will take you to myself, so that where I am, there you may be also. And you know the way to the place where I am going." Thomas said to him, "Lord, we do not know where you are going. How can we know the way?" Jesus said to him, "I am the way, and the truth, and the life. No

one comes to the Father except through me. If you know me, you will know my Father also. From now on you do know him and have seen him."

Do not let your hearts be troubled, says Jesus to his disciples who he is about to inform about his impending "departure." He is letting them know, I, the Spirit-bearer you have been hoping for, am about to "leave" you—which, of course, would be troubling to disciples who thought the one they were hoping for would come and establish an everlasting kingdom. He's not supposed to leave. He's supposed to rule. Aside from showing signs, Jesus hasn't quite gotten started yet, as far as these disciples are concerned, because Rome still lords over them. Yet, part of the reason the disciples should not be troubled that Jesus is "leaving" is because *In my Father's house there are many dwelling places,* and when Jesus "leaves" he will be going for their sakes, or, to *prepare a place for you.* Let me pause here to rearrange our mental blueprints that tend to obscure a passage such as this. When Jesus says there are many dwelling places in the Father's house, he is not saying that he is going to go to a place in the sky called heaven that has big mansions; nor is Jesus saying that he is going to a specific mansion that belongs to God to go and do some housekeeping as he awaits their arrival when they die.

The Father's house is not a massive brick-laden or stucco-sprayed house, nor is it a reference for many such mansions. Rather, the Father's house can be understood in a variety of ways that name the same glorious reality. Jesus is going to be *in* the Father or live *in* the Father's embrace. Put differently, it's a qualitative intimacy of oneness that Jesus is going to enjoy with the Father. That could sound a bit like a selfish thing for Jesus to say to a people who are distressed, especially when this is the same Jesus who empties himself of this privileged status for our sake (Phil 2). But the good news is that the embrace of the Father is very roomy, so there is not only room for Jesus but also "many dwelling places" meaning that there's room for all of us in the Father's embrace. Jesus is "leaving" not to enjoy that intimacy for his own sake, but when he goes, he takes his humanity and so all of us with him.

This is where Christology as briefly laid out becomes essential. We noted earlier that Jesus is not merely a human being, but humanity itself, so that what happens to him transforms and happens to all of humanity.

Because Jesus is fully God and fully man, and therefore simultaneously Jesus of Nazareth and the Son of God, Jesus going to the Father *is* Jesus taking humanity itself to the Father. That very act makes it possible for us to enjoy the same intimacy that he does with the Father. That's what it means for Jesus to prepare a place for us in the Father's house. However, Jesus not only brings us with him to the Father; he also promises to come to us. *And if I go prepare a place for you, I will come again and will take you to myself, so that where I am, there you will be also.* In this context, when Jesus says "I will come again" he is not referring to his eschatological "second coming" at all. The context is fitted to the promise of the Holy Spirit, *And I will ask the Father, and he will give you another Advocate, to be with you forever. This is the Spirit of truth, whom the world cannot receive, because it neither sees him nor knows him. You know him, because he abides with you, and he will be in you.* The sending of the Spirit is the very Spirit of Jesus whereby he can guarantee that *I will not leave you orphaned; I am coming to you.* The physical presence of Jesus will no longer be seen by the world because he will be "gone" as far as they're concerned. But those who discern the deeper truth of resurrection and ascension will know that Pentecost is nothing less than Jesus himself being present to the world not as merely as *a* person, but through a community of prophets to whom he has radically and ontologically joined himself—to the community he is at-one-ed with.

While Jesus is present to the Father by being in his intimate embrace at his ascension, he pours out his Spirit to remain *physically* present to us and to the world by forming a community of prophets to be the very body of Christ on the earth. Hence, *in a little while* (at my death, resurrection, and ascension) *the world will no longer see me, but you will see me; because I live, you will also live. On that day you will know that I am in my Father, and you in me, and I in you.*

When Jesus ascends:

1. He is in the Father.
2. We are in Jesus.
3. Jesus sends the Spirit so that simultaneous to items 1 and 2, Jesus and the Father are in us.

There is so much going on between John 14–17 that can fill many theses. For the purposes of this book, I will simply note that when Jesus goes to the Father at his ascension, he makes room for us by the Spirit. That same Spirit that makes room for us in the Father is given to us and joins us so intimately with Jesus that we will be called the body of Christ. The Spirit is not only Jesus coming to us, but when he comes to us, the Father is in him. Let me put it this way: The Spirit makes it possible for us to be *in* Christ so that when Christ goes to the Father, we too go with him as there is plenty of room for us. Therefore, we are simultaneously *in* the Father *and* in the Son. It doesn't stop there for I only named what happens at ascension. At Pentecost, the Spirit that joins us intimately to the Father and the Son gets poured out so that both the Father and the Son come to be *in* us as well. Hence, we are in the Son and the Father by the Spirit, and by that same Spirit being poured out, the Father and the Son are also in us.

This would be impossible if God were not the one triune God. Hence the doctrine of the Trinity is not a mathematical problem to solved, but the gloriously good news that we share in the intimacy and glory that Jesus and the Father shared before the world existed (John 17:5).

It's no wonder we are repeatedly called the body of Christ. This is one of those phrases that we have become so accustomed to in church culture that the reality it bespeaks no longer hits us as radically as it should. When Scripture says that we are the body of Christ, it means it in a very real and ontological sense. I often ask my students if they believe that the ascended Christ makes himself physically available to us today. That if I wanted to see and touch him physically, would I be able to do that? After some prodding, most answer yes, to which I ask a follow-up question: Where has he made himself available for me to see and touch? Scripture does not flinch as we do. As Saul is heading to Damascus to carry out the orders of an edict from the high priest in Jerusalem to arrest the followers of Jesus, we read that "suddenly a light from heaven flashed around him. He fell to the ground and heard a voice saying to him, 'Saul, Saul, why do you persecute *me*?'" Notice, this is the ascended Jesus speaking about the community he has poured out his Spirit upon. Saul had no access to Jesus's ascended bodily presence in the way that we imagine a bodily presence—as an individual among other individuals. Yet, Jesus did not ask Saul "why are you persecuting *my people*," but "*me*." What you do to the body of Christ, you do to Jesus himself.

Scripture and the ancient Christian tradition who lived in it are quite straightforward and unreserved when it comes to claiming that God shares the relational oneness he has within himself with his people. This oneness is emphatic, to point where we are *in* the triune God, and the triune God is simultaneously *in* us (John 17:20-23). Despite the fact that Scripture and tradition do not shy away from identifying God's action and story with that of his people, our modern Western Christian ears hear that as deeply problematic at best, or heretical at worst.

"That sounds like heresy!" proclaimed one of my students. This was in response to me when I quoted someone who was integral to formulating what we now take for granted as orthodox trinitarian doctrine. Let me say that again, one of my theology students thought that a key idea stated by a *pillar of Christian orthodoxy* said something heretical. We're far too comfortable and even proud of being ahistorical, thinking it's possible to understand Scripture faithfully apart from the primal Christian communities that gifted us these texts. I will speak more on this in chapters 7 and 8. The genius of the ancient writer I quoted to my troubled student has given Christians the framework to boldly proclaim that Jesus of Nazareth and the Father aren't merely *like* each other, but perfectly share the same essence. Jesus is not *like*

PART I | (RE)INTERPRETING THE WORLD

God, he *is* God. It's the reason why Christians aren't idolators for worshipping Jesus.

When I teach on how God relates to his creatures, I often like to give quotes without naming the source just to see how my students will react. It's funny, and frankly concerning, how our modern piety shaped by our inherited philosophies make us uncomfortable with orthodox Christianity. Put more starkly, we're so comfortable and at home with our inherited unfaithful understandings of a non-trinitarian God, that when we hear orthodox teaching on the triune God and its implications for creation, it sounds like heresy. Again, I will unpack how this happened in more detail in Part II of this work, but for now, let me just drop the quote and the name. The quote I shared was: "God became man so that man might become god." The one who said this was none other than a pillar of orthodox trinitarian theology and a major reason you and I believe Jesus is fully God and fully man. He did the heavy lifting for Christology with special emphasis on the incarnation and was a great and essential bishop of the early church: Athanasius of Alexandria (293–373).[4] I will say much more about him and take a close look at how he reads Scripture in chapter 7.

Back to the biblical text. Where does Luke get off claiming in the voice of the ascended Christ that what one does to Jesus's people one also does to Jesus himself? Recount the story of Scripture through the lens of the Spirit we just discussed. The story of Scripture does not begin with a Greek-like mythological tale of how gods lived and acted in the heavens "before" or "above" the creation of this world. There is no account of Yahweh's power and authority by way of God being "in heaven" ruling over other gods. Rather, the revealed history of an eternal God and the history of finite creatures are told together. The English Bible can't even let out a full sentence without the mention of God *with* creatures and proceeds to tell the whole story from that vantage. "In the beginning *God created* . . ." Further, God is revealed as a talkative God

---

4. His "God became man . . ." quote appears in his *On the Incarnation*. A more recent translation puts it: "For he was incarnate that we might be made god." See Athanasius, *On the Incarnation*, 107.

who moves history forward by introducing himself—and continually speaking to Abram, to Moses, and lurching history forward by filling people with his future-creating, life-bringing Spirit. For Israel, God is known by his acts in history as the one who delivered them from Egypt. For the primal church, this same God who delivered Israel from Egypt has now raised Jesus from dead. Thus, God is known by his acts in history.

Does Jesus share our nervousness about the divine relating to creatures too intimately? Hardly. Twice in Matthew 25 (vv. 40, 45), when exhorting his disciples for treating him well, he identifies with the hungry, thirsty, stranger, unclothed, ill, or the prisoner: "Whatever you do to the least of these who are members of my family, you did it to me" (Matt 25:40). There is some debate as to whether Jesus is talking about people in general who are hungry, thirst, etc. or whether he is specifically talking about his followers (read: "who are family members," or "brothers and sisters of mine") who are poor and/or have been imprisoned for their faith. I tend to think the latter. But the point I am drawing out here is how even prior to his resurrection, ascension, and Pentecost, he's already identifying with his people. After breathing his Spirit on the disciples, he sends them by the Spirit as the Father has sent him, leaving the power of his forgiveness (at least partially) in the hands of his people (John 20:23).

The effect of this teaching, far from producing pride, should produce fear and trembling. The church being Christ's physical availability to the world imposes a great responsibility that I would rather be without. For example, Paul reminds the Corinthians of their being profoundly united with Jesus as grounds for a stern and shocking rebuke. "Do you not know that your bodies are members of Christ? Should I therefore take the members of Christ and make them members of a prostitute? Never! Do you not know that whoever is united to a prostitute becomes one body with her?" (1 Cor 6:15–16). Did you catch that? The Corinthian church is so identified with Christ that if its members who are members of Christ copulate with a prostitute, it's not that the sin will cause them to cease to be members of Christ's body, but rather that they are so joined to Christ that what they do, they make Christ do.

Simply put, if we use our identity with Christ to love, forgive, heal, and prophesy, that is Christ acting in the world through his people. Jesus keeps this relation to us even at cost to himself. Christ is so joined to us that when we are persecuted by Saul, he does not retreat from us but is also persecuted. On the other hand, when we join ourselves to prostitutes, or refuse to forgive people, he still does not retreat from us, but rather, we make him do it. But thanks be to God that what he touches is overwhelmed by his holiness. Nor does the unholy or unclean tarnish him. He is God, after all. This is the witness of his ministry. That said, the theological reality that we are one with Christ, and are his physical availability in and to the world, when properly understood, does not produce pride but praise. "For from him and through him and to him are all things. To him be the glory forever. Amen." (Rom 11:36).

Conclusion

At Pentecost, Jesus fulfills his promise in John that he will not leave us orphaned. He thus creates a community of prophets to be his physical and embodied presence for the sake of the world. Prior to that movement, when Jesus ascends as humanity itself, he brings us with him to enjoy the intimacy he shares with the Father. That is what it means for Jesus to prepare a place for us in the Father, by the Spirit. While Jesus prepares a place for us in the Father, the Holy Spirit at Pentecost is the down payment as we wait for the full actuality of being joined to God with resurrected bodies that are made to bear that glory.

Pentecost is not only about God giving us a foretaste of the fullness that lies ahead of us as we live in "the last days." It is also about the empowerment of believers to participate in Jesus's mission *as* Jesus in bringing others into that life. This is the church's mission. That said, let me remind readers of what I have so far laid out regarding the Spirit in the story of Scripture.

- From the beginning, the Spirit is the very life-animating wind and breath of God.
- The life-giving Spirit creates history when coming upon prophets to bring about change with their speech and action. By the Spirit, some of the speak promises on God's behalf.
- As Israel loses hope in this-worldly solutions to their alienation from God, their hope becomes aimed at the world to come. The promises from the mouth of her prophets turn toward awaiting a Spirit-bearer who will pour out the Spirit he bears to create a community of prophets.
- Jesus is identified as that Spirit-bearer in the New Testament. His life, words, and testimony are the very Spirit of prophecy.
- Jesus resurrects and ascends to the embrace of the Father with death behind him. He goes there not only for his sake but to prepare a place for us to share in that intimacy.
- Pentecost creates a community of prophets, making us Jesus's physical presence on earth for the sake of missionally bringing others into the kingdom, until Jesus appears in glory to judge the living and the dead.

PART II

The Myths That Have Severed God from Creatures

IN PART I, I aimed to retrieve the centrality of community, story, and the Christian vision of God-with-us for the sake of moving toward recovering at least portions of our ancient Christian identity. The Holy Spirit joins us to God, to each other, and to our shared story's eschatological fulfillment in God.

If it is true that this vision of the triune God-with-us is at home in ancient Christian worship, and thus within the reading of her Scriptures, how have we lost touch with that vision? Moreover, how have we become so radically individualistic in our understanding of what it means to be human? How have we become storyless while worshipping a distant monad in the sky who must "intervene" in a world otherwise separate from him? In other words, how have we come to tacitly think of ourselves as individuals, and of God as a non-triune being among beings? How have these questions become superfluous in our imaginations when reflecting on questions like these was the center for Christian thought and practice for most of our history?

In Part II, readers will receive an account of how we have ended up with the need to reconstruct and creatively retrieve an ancient Christian vision for the sake of our future in the first place. We will address all these questions by first looking at how early

Christian worship was practiced: invoking the triune God-with-us who first claimed the church as his own. That will be the purpose of chapter 6, where we will take a close look at what the church is and how its message creates practices that serve as the incubator for its identity as the body of Christ. In chapter 7, I show how the worship of the church worked itself out in the church's explicit thought-life about God and creatures. I will do so by noting how these practices also shaped the way early Christians read Scripture in a way informed by a trinitarian understanding of God. In chapter 8, I will sketch three shifts that changed the way Christians understood worship, its means of knowing truth, its means of salvation, and its understanding of God. The consequences of these shifts are still with us today.

CHAPTER 6

A Fitting Place for God

The Church is not simply an institution. She is a "mode of existence," a way of being. The mystery of the Church, even in its institutional dimension, is deeply bound to the being of man, to the being of the world and to the very being of God.

–JOHN ZIZIOULAS

THE FEARS OF THE CHURCH succumbing to culture ought to be unnecessary, for when the church is being faithful to itself, it creates and nurtures its own culture. The church ought to create a culture that forms personal identities through communal practices like baptizing, prayer, the laying on of hands, eating and drinking, teaching, and reading. These practices create a context for Christians to develop ways of being, thinking, and acting in the world. This is a simple claim, but it is far from a boring or inconsequential one.

At its best, the church forms me to act and think like a Christian in a world that tacitly and explicitly tries to form me to think otherwise. Part of thinking like a Christian is learning to read the Bible like one. Remember, Christianity is a *received* faith. It is a gift from the triune God who has created a community we call the church. If this is true, then it is worth our efforts to rediscover precisely:

1. What kind of a community the church is.
2. What the central content of its message is.
3. What practices and habits of speech communicate its message and form its messengers.
4. How the previous items create the context for engaging Scripture in developing Christian theology (the topic of next chapter).

This chapter will unpack these first three items.

THE MESSAGE THAT CREATES THE CHURCH

"If Christ has not been raised, then our proclamation has been in vain, and your faith has been in vain" (1 Cor 15:14). The uniqueness of the church is that it is formed around an unprecedented event supposed to have happened with Jesus. What exactly is unique about Jesus and the event that happened with him? It is not that he claimed to be some kind of messianic king. There have been many figures throughout the world's history who have made similar claims to be *the* king who would establish a kingdom on this earth that would somehow be without end. Nor is Jesus the first and only person to be killed for supposed heresy by the hands of the religious powers. Nor was he the only would-be revolutionary or criminal who died on a Roman cross for being a threat to the established kingdom. Nor are Jesus's claims to be in some way divine unique to him, as emperors and other teachers would make similar claims about themselves. What, then, was it that made the life and death of Jesus in any way consequential for the world? If not the claims just mentioned, nor the kind of death he suffered that is unique to Jesus, what is it? The answer to that question is the very event that creates the church.

The church exists because, and *only* because, a particular event happened in history. *Jesus was raised from the dead.* This was indeed a unique one-off event. Jesus's being risen is nothing like what happened with Lazarus or the little boy that Elijah raised in

2 Kings 4 (or other such similar events in the Bible). When they were raised, they were brought back into the same reality in which they died. While Lazarus and the little boy had experienced a real death, they were merely resuscitated back into the same reality with non-transfigured bodies that remained subject to decay. Their resuscitations did not defeat death, they merely postponed it. Despite being brought back to life, death remained ahead of them.

The uniqueness of Jesus's resurrection is that he was raised into a *new* life, one where death is defeated. Death had been *the* defining problem for all creation. It determined the parameters of all that existed, setting concrete limits to all creaturely reality. Death seemingly held sway over all creation before the resurrection of Jesus. Now that he is risen, a new creation has been inaugurated in which death no longer has the final word over all living things. It is no longer death that determines the limits of creation's existence, it is the resurrection of Jesus that frees creation from those limits. All of creation has now been opened to new possibilities beyond death. Put simply, it is no longer death, but the life of Jesus that determines the deepest truth for all reality.

So then, what kind of community is the church? It is a community formed by and gathered around a particular piece of good news: The Father has raised Jesus from the dead by the power of the Holy Spirit. Death has lost. Or, in short, *Jesus is risen*. That is the gospel (good news). If that event did not happen, there is no reason for the church to exist. While the world still lives with the fears of decay, through its speech and practices:

- The church exists as it communicates to each other both in reminder and *formation*: "Jesus is risen!"
- The church lives as it communicates to the world in *proclamation*: "Jesus is risen!"
- The church simply is a community whose shared life puts on full display the fact that death has lost because Jesus is risen.

The people who constitute the church live and "die" as though that message is true. The risen Christ is Lord; therefore, death does not have the final say for all creation. Nor do earthly kings and kingdoms have the final say over our lives.

The church's communal life communicates that Jesus is risen, both within through reminder and formation, and to the world in proclamation. But what does it look like for a community to exist as though the living risen Lord of all creation is *presently* reigning? Jesus is not a relic of the past. His life is not frozen between the first few decades of the first century. Jesus is nothing like a dead loved one who has passed away, who we merely remember in our hearts as an item of our collective pasts. In our cultural imaginations, our dead loved ones are now inaccessible or unavailable to us. We only hope to someday be reunited with them "in heaven." However, this is not how the church is to relate to Jesus.

Jesus is alive. He is not a mere memory. To be a living person is to be *presently* available to other living persons. To be alive is to be available to address others and be addressed by them. Living persons can be heard, spoken to, touched, embraced, and seen; living persons don't merely respond, they initiate. On the other hand, to be dead is to be unavailable and inaccessible in all of these ways. Because Jesus is not dead, he is indeed bodily available both to us and to the world, here and now.

GOD FINDS A PLACE IN HISTORY

While all Christian churches profess belief in the risen Christ, the present-ness of Jesus is a real problem to our modernistic imaginations. This is especially true when we aren't explicitly reshaped around trinitarian worship. The modern mind boggles when attempting to make sense of how God can be tangibly present with us while remaining omnipresent and transcendent at the same time. However, I suggest that when our minds are shaped by worshiping and addressing the triune God by the Spirit in conversation with our ancient faith and practices, it becomes less difficult to see—albeit no less mysterious. Christian worship recognizes that while God is Lord over history, we know him as he is made present in our midst.

If the God of Scripture is the triune God-with-us, as we have been arguing throughout this book, then God *happens* in history. In other words, God can be identified by his acts within it. To recall some previous points, God is not primarily known through mythical stories of defeating other gods in the heavenlies "before" or "outside" of time. Rather, he is known by the history he lives with his creatures. God speaks to Abraham and acts in and among his family, and so they know him. God makes promises to Israel, acts among them, and delivers them from Egypt, and so they know him. His ultimate self-disclosure comes through Jesus, primarily affirmed by the historical event of his life, death, and resurrection. The acts of God are at once historical *and more* than historical, but never less.

If Christians are right about God's presence on earth, then Christianity confronts the standard religious impulses for what it means to know God. In fact, early Christian thinkers were ridiculed for just how material and embodied their worship and thought-life was. The first systematic critique of Christianity was given by a man in the first century named Celsus who thought it nonsense that "God" should "leave his own abode" to come to us. This would fundamentally undo the structure of the universe as he understood it. "God," thought Celsus, must remain untouched by creaturely reality and the goings on of history. "God" must be accessible only through the mind purging itself of what it sees in the world of senses. "God" must not be said to be fully present and revealed in history, lest he be understood to abandon his serene "abode" away from creatures.

An early and thorough Christian response to such critiques was given by Origen of Alexandria (c. 185–254). In providing a Christian response to Celsus, Origen points him to Jeremiah 23:24, in which God is said to fill heaven and earth such that when he acts in history, God does not "vacate his own seat, so that one place should be empty of him, and another which did not formerly contain him be filled. But the power and divinity of God comes through him whom God chooses, and resides in him in whom *it finds a place*, not changing its situation, nor leaving its own place empty and filling another."[1] In other words, because God fills all, he doesn't need to travel to get from one place to another.

Because God is triune, he can be the Creator and Lord *over* history, *and* he can act *within* history without abandoning his "abode." God can:

- Talk to the patriarchs, prophets, and others in Scripture by coming to them as the "Word of the Lord."
- Talk to Moses as "the burning bush."
- Abide in the ark of the covenant.

He can do all of this and more in history while not abandoning his transcendence over it. When dedicating the temple to God, despite Solomon's recognition that "even heaven and the highest heaven cannot contain you, much less this house that I have built," he prays that God would set his eyes and name in it (1 Kgs 8). We then discover that the same glory that fills heaven and earth can also fill that which was built by human hands (2 Chr 7). In these texts, Solomon dares to ask God to be especially present in a particular place in history by drawing on the faithfulness of God who makes promises and keeps them. Going back to Origen, God is present in history where he chooses and where he *finds a place* through the communities, lives, and spaces we create for and around him. He does so without being "less" present over history in his "abode." God is a talkative God in history and because he is faithful to keep his promises, he will be who he will be in history as he simultaneously lords from beyond it. He will be precisely where he chooses to be, promises to be, and where he finds a place while simultaneously being the one in whom we live and move and have our being.

For the Christian, the real question isn't whether God makes himself bodily and particularly available, but where and how? Where does the triune God in Christ promise to be present? Where does he find a place? I will recall some points made in previous

---

1. Origen, *Contra Celsum* IV.5.

chapters and add some specifics regarding Christ's embodiment in Christian worship.

GOD FINDS A PLACE IN COMMUNAL PRACTICES

Once again, the church exists as it lives in accordance with the fact that Jesus is risen. He is indeed bodily available both to us and to the world, here and now. That said, if the Son of the Father is alive and present by the power of the Holy Spirit, where and *how* is he bodily available?[2] As discussed in the previous chapter, the New Testament and ancient church were quite straightforward on this. Simply put, Jesus is physically available as the church—the body to which Jesus has joined himself by the power of the Spirit.

The day of Pentecost actualizes the union between Jesus and his followers in a profound way, making us a community of prophets bearing the very Spirit of Jesus. Just so, we are the body of Christ, and what is done to us is done to Christ. Paul says that God has made Christ "the head over all things for the church, which is his body, the fullness of him who fills all in all" (Eph 1:22–23; cf. 4:15–16). On this side of the eschaton, we know this by faith as we *practice the truth of our union with the Son—invoking the Holy Spirit in our worship to make Christ present to us*. One day, that faith will become sight when Christ is fully and finally all in all. For now, by faith we know that:

- Jesus sends the Spirit to make his followers one as the Father and the Son are one (John 17).
- Jesus sends the Spirit so that he might be nearer to us at his resurrection and ascension (John 14).
- Jesus sends the Spirit that is poured out on Pentecost (Acts 2).

The Spirit of Jesus is the down payment of our future-coming promise. The Spirit of Jesus is the eschatological Spirit that will make Christ *fully* present to us at the end of the ages. The unstinting presence of Jesus will be seen and experienced at the end of

2. Recall chapter 5 on this point.

the ages. It is this reality that Augustine called the *totus Christus*, or the total Christ. This simply names the reality of the fulfillment and consummation of Jesus being fully joined and *at-one-ed* with his creatures and so all creation. This reality is precisely what Christians mean by heaven. Heaven is not so much a place, but a qualitative union with the triune God.

Prior to our ultimate fulfillment in and as the *totus Christus*, then, where do Christians find the physical body of Jesus here and now? If Christians want to know where Jesus is bodily accessible to them in the present, we look at and engage:

1. Their brothers and sisters with whom they are gathered in worship.
2. The altar that holds the body and blood of Jesus.

Item number one has already been covered in the previous chapter. I want to spend some time here talking about item two. The altar that holds the body and blood of Jesus has historically been the center of Christian worship. Furthermore, it has been essential to church's identity and our salvation. Worship, identity, and salvation were intricately connected for the ancient church. It is primarily in and through Jesus's communal body that in Christ, the triune God speaks to us, hears us, touches us, and we respond in kind. *Christian worship is where the triune God-with-us is invoked and made visible both to ourselves and to the world around us.* This is not a new or controversial claim, although it is one that we have lost touch with. If Christian worship is "ground zero" for where Jesus is bodily available to speak and be spoken to, then it is worth our efforts to unpack just how the apostolic churches understood the presentness of the triune God, through Christ, in their worship.

GOD SAVES WITH HUMAN PRACTICES

For the ancient church, the present-ness of the triune God through the risen Christ in worship mattered. Indeed, it had everything to do with salvation. If Jesus is not present in our worship by the

Holy Spirit, then we are not joined to the God who saves. Thus, in early Christian worship, there was a very close and interdependent relationship between (1) the Trinity, (2) worship, and (3) salvation.

Trinity: For the ancient church, Father, Son, and Holy Spirit were not three names for one God, but *one* personal proper name for the Christian God who gives himself for us. It's the name of the God who draws us into his bountiful and capacious life. God loves creatures so much that he draws us into his own life even at his own cost. On the creaturely side of this reality, being joined to God happens when we join ourselves to those Christ has identified as his body. The primal act through which people are brought into the fellowship of believers and simultaneously into fellowship with God, is by being initiated into the name: Father, Son, and Holy Spirit. Not only were Christians initiated into this name through baptism, but they were also sustained by the God who bears that triune name through a variety of practices, some of which will be named below.

Worship (Regula Fidei): The church, however, did not merely have a threefold name for her triune God. It also had descriptions which identified the acts of each person that constituted that one name. These identifying descriptions came to be known as the "rule of faith," which was essential for early Christian worship. In its earliest stages, the rule of faith was not fixed in writing. Rather, the rule of faith was a set of speech habits and practices that formed the earliest Christian communities. These communities did not have to wonder whether or not they were being true to apostolic faith, they simply were those communities planted by the apostles and led by those apostolically appointed. The practices and speech habits of those communities created an incubated "culture" where the triune God was named and worshipped for his acts in and among them. Those practices were commonly that of:

1. *Catechesis*: introductory teaching of the Christian faith so that those who were candidates to be baptized knew into which God and into which faith they were to be baptized.

2. *Baptism*: the public and embodied act by which the candidate is joined to the church, and therefore to Christ's death and resurrection—done in the name of the Father, Son, and Holy Spirit.

3. *Liturgy*: ordered worship that culminated at the table of the Lord, where Christ and his people are visibly and explicitly joined together. The entire service leading up to that event was preparation for that embodied union with the triune God.

4. *Preaching*: always assumed and aimed at proclaiming that the Father has raised Jesus from the dead by the power of the Holy Spirit. Texts were read and sermons were preached to proclaim that very event. The reading of Scripture and the faithful preaching of the gospel were understood as the living voice of Jesus in our midst.

5. *Exorcisms*: demons were cast out of people in the name of the Father, Son, and Holy Spirit, demonstrating that the triune God presently reigns over the kingdom of darkness and the gods of this world.

6. *Polemics*: when false teaching about Jesus emerged, it was often rooted in a picture of the world where God and humanity cannot interpenetrate. The triune God as worshiped by the Christian church was essential to keep the people of God from swaying from its Christian vision of the world.

In each of these practices, it is explicitly the triune God who is addressed. When the apostles and their disciples had long been dead, the rule of faith became fixed in texts known as creeds. These creeds were confessed in tandem with the reading of Scripture for the sake of Christian formation. Most of the Christian church still recites these creeds in our worship today. They are gifts that provide the church the apostolic understanding of who God is and of his tri-personal acts among us.

Salvation: The descriptions of the personal acts of the triune God that we see in the early creeds are not random. They name the *salvific* acts of Father, Son, and Holy Spirit. They put on full display that the triune God has a favorable disposition toward his creation and that favorable disposition undergirds his saving acts toward it, even at cost to himself. What it meant for an act of God to be salvific had little to do with "going to heaven when you die." That's almost exclusively what we mean by "salvation" today. However, for the ancient Christian community, God could address them, and they could address God. It is through that present communion with him that he is joined to the church, and the church to him. Worship was about being made present before Jesus and making Jesus present before them. It was about being available to Jesus to be a place where the divine can "find its place," to borrow from the words of Origen. Christ finding his place among and within us through Christian worship is nothing less than being joined to the triune God.

The act of being joined to God in prayer, worship, and church practice *is* our salvation. As Gregory of Nazianzus puts it: "For that which He has not assumed He has not healed; *That which is united to the Godhead is saved.*"[3] For the Nazianzen, when Jesus took on flesh in the incarnation, he assumed humanity in himself that he might save it. Christian worship is our participation in being united to the God who is Father, Son, and Holy Spirit. In worship, we say "yes" to the union made possible by God himself. Another name for that "yes" is invocation.

Conclusion

For the ancient church, salvation means being united and brought into the life of the triune God. Union with God was made possible by God bountifully giving himself in the Son through the Spirit. The resurrection means that not even death can stop that fellowship, and so the triune God is presently available to be addressed and to address us in worship. When the church addresses God, we *invoke* him. By that invocation, the triune God who saves is

---

3. Gregory of Nazianzus, *Against Apollinarius,* Epistle 101.

made present. Like Solomon, the church recognizes that God is ubiquitous yet makes himself presently available precisely because he promised he would be with us. We invoke God in worship to make the Lord of history present with us. We are the body of Christ where he chooses to be and thus *finds a place* in us, with us, and among us. We don't bear God for ourselves, but like Christ, we bear him for the sake of the world.

That's really all that invocation means—acknowledging the availability of Christ and embodying that present availability in our worship. When we invoke the triune God, we acknowledge that Christ is speaking to us, and so we speak back to him. When we invoke the triune God, we acknowledge that Christ is bodily present both *to* us and *in* us by eating the bread and drinking the wine in which he promised to be present. At the table of the Lord, we eat the risen deified body of Christ where God "plants himself, in accordance with His plan of grace, in all believers by means of that Flesh, which derives its subsistence from both wine and bread, mingling Himself with the bodies of believers, in order that, by union with that which is immortal, man might also participate in incorruption."[4]

We communicate with our bodies through these practices, both to ourselves and to the world, that the risen Christ is present with us and in us. By his Holy Spirit, we are indeed not orphans, but the triune God has joined himself to us and us to him, here and now. That union of God with his creatures is our salvation. By the Spirit we are being saved into an inheritance that we have now by faith, but that union will one day become sight.

---

4. Gregory of Nyssa, *Catechetical Oration* 98.1–6.

CHAPTER 7

The God Who Refuses Safe Distances

Beloved, we are God's children now; what we will be has not yet been revealed. What we do know is this: when he is revealed, we will be like him, for we will see him as he is.

—1 JOHN 3:2–3

For now we see in a mirror, dimly, but then we will see face to face. Now I know only in part; then I will know fully, even as I have been fully known.

—1 CORINTHIANS 13:12

IN THE PREVIOUS CHAPTER, I discussed that the explicit invocation of the triune God was ever-present in the ancient worship of the common Christian. Theology could not be separated from Christian worship, and neither could the reading and hearing of the Christian Scriptures. Worship was shaped around the naming and calling upon the God who is Father, Son, and Holy Spirit. This naturally gave way to important questions by reflective Christian worshipers. How can the threefold name be addressing a God who is tri-personal, yet simultaneously perfectly one? Christian invocation pressed the church for conceptually faithful ways of talking about the very nature of God who joined himself to them in worship.

The task of thinking about ways of faithfully talking about the nature of the triune God became more crucial as the church moved through time. Indeed, it was of principal importance. If it turns out that God is not triune, then Christians are idolators. Why? Because Christians claim that to worship Jesus is to worship God himself. Moreover, if God is not triune, being joined to Christ by the power of the Holy Spirit is not the same as being joined to God. This is a big deal. If Jesus can't fully join me to God, this is another way of saying that Jesus can't save us.

As the church moved through time, she found herself distanced from her now long-deceased original founders, and popular religious and pagan impulses of the day continued to press themselves on the church's imagination. These impulses created assumptions that started to shape the way some people understood the nature of the Christian God, while also impacting how they read the church's Scriptures. These presuppositions couldn't be fully ignored, and neither could they be fully adopted. Rather, they had to be *gospelized* by a people formed not by the reigning common sense of the day, but by Christian worship. Without proper formation, the religious presuppositions of the day would serve as lenses through which to read Scripture. If presuppositions inherited from outside of Christian worship go unchecked when reading Scripture, then the Bible itself can be used to and undo the teaching of the church. This is exactly what (almost) happened.

PROTECTING GOD FROM CREATURES

In the philosophical and religious imagination of the ancient world outside of Christian worship, there were many mistaken attempts to make sense of Jesus and his relationship to God. For the sake of time and space, I will briefly touch on one popular version. Remember in the last chapter when I discussed Celsus's objections to the Christian claim that in Christ, God himself is with us? Celsus argued that God can't "leave his abode" to become a creature in a world subjected to death and decay. That thought wasn't unique to Celsus. God and creation being set at odds was prevalent in the common sense of the ancient world. Christian worship presented a radical break from the worldview of its time, hence Christianity was the object of much ridicule in the ancient world, as I have noted in previous chapters. For the pagan imagination, what makes God *the* God is that he is utterly untouched by the created world of change.

Keeping creation at a comfortable distance from God understandably infiltrated the imagination of some leaders in the worshiping Christian community. It was so embedded in the religious imagination that Christians continued to be tempted by it. One major theological heresy was taught by a group who came to be known as the Arians—named after one of its chief proponents, a presbyter named Arius (c. 256–336). Basically, Arians taught that Jesus is not *the* God in the full sense. Instead, the Arians taught that God created the Son, and through the created Son, God brought about the rest of creation. In that model, Jesus is a creature of God, albeit an elevated one. As such, "God himself" can remain unsullied by a created reality subjected to decay, while a semi-divine Jesus can enter and experience the world of change without introducing change or suffering into God "himself." In this picture, what is divine remains safely protected and untouched by creaturely reality.

Before you cast stones at the "obvious" errors of the Arians, in the time in which these ideas arose, they were not so obviously wrong. They were tempting. They were popular. They made sense of the kind of difference between creator and creature that was common in the ancient world. Moreover, much to the horror of our modern Christian practice that imagines that reading the Bible privately keeps us from all error, Arius can be said to be thoroughly "biblical" in the sense that we mean it today.

When the conventional and common-sensically assumed philosophies, wisdom, pious impulses, and methods for understanding truth go unchecked, we can read Scripture with conventional assumptions and imagine that we're merely following what the Bible plainly says. We think that by doing so, we're protected from deception. Using Scripture in this way is not new. As we will see, it has been happening throughout history. But what is the fruit of such reading and understanding?

THE "CLEAR" DISTANCE BETWEEN FATHER AND SON

If I were to ask a Christian today what it is that keeps them from serious theological error, I can almost guarantee that the vast majority would simply reply, "The Bible." All one needs to do is read the Bible alone and that is our sure way to keep all major error at bay (like the Bereans!). Much of this naivete has to do with being blissfully unaware of how heresies came to be. In the same way that in our popular imagination we tend to imagine Satan in an unsophisticated and almost cartoonish fashion, we think the same about heterodox thinkers. We imagine them as careless in their thought and wholly unconcerned with orthodoxy—seeking only to sabotage orthodox Christian thought and worship in its infancy. But when thinking through the more popular and tempting heresies that were serious threats for the ancient church, nothing could be further from the truth. *They weren't trying to be heretics; they were trying to be biblical.*

Today, we hold to certain assumptions about Scripture that were not assumed by its ancient Christian tradents and readers. For example, in our churches today it is a basic principle that Scripture is "clear" and "plain" regarding the things that "really" matter for salvation and instruction. Yet, if we assume that what we dogmatically hold to is "clear" by following what Scripture "plainly" says, the conversation between Athanasius and Arius at a crucial point in the development of the church will challenge that assumption.

Drawing on their anxieties of keeping God separate and free from creatures, an Arian can point to the various texts where Jesus "clearly" asserts a difference between himself and the Father. However, the kind of separation between the Father and the Son that the Arian reading of Scripture called for was one that would undermine orthodox Christian worship. But a glaring problem remains: the Arian position is in alignment with a "plain" reading of Scripture. Indeed, this gap between the Father and the Son can be discerned through a straightforward reading of Jesus's own words. For example, in Scripture, Jesus seems to assert the differences between himself and the Father at multiple levels. Explicitly, Jesus talked about how he and Father differed in their:

Knowledge: The Father knows things that the Son does not.

- "But about that day and hour no one knows, neither the angels of heaven, nor the Son, but only the Father" (Matt 24:36).

Goodness: The Father is good to a degree that the Son is not.

- "Why do you call *me* good?" asks Jesus. He answers his own rhetorical question by saying, "No one is good except God (ὁ Θεός[1]) alone" (Mark 10:18; Luke 18:19).

Wills: The Father can will things that the Son does not. At the garden of Gethsemane, their wills are not only different, but at odds.

- "Not my [Jesus's] will, but yours [the Father's] be done." (Luke 22:42).

On the face of these texts, Jesus is "clearly" drawing a hard-and-fast line between him and the Father. It is a biblically clear line to which Arians would like to remain faithful. From Jesus's own words in Scripture, we can plainly discern a stark enough difference between the Father and the Son to warrant the kind of separation between them that Christians vehemently opposed. Indeed, these differences are profoundly consequential. How can

---

1. *ho Theos: the* God. That is, God in the *absolute* sense.

distinctions of knowledge, goodness, and will intelligibly be said to exist in one perfectly unified life?

Given what Jesus has said in these texts, what are we to make of Christian dogma that asserts the non-explicitly biblical notion of the Father and the Son being co-equal and co-eternal? In what "biblically clear" sense—insofar as we depend on explicit prooftexts—can we say that the Son is "of one being/substance with the Father" as Christian dogma insists? Not even John 1:1 makes a clear assertion on this matter. Early Christian thinkers did not point to this passage as a proof, and that was for good reason. I won't give in to the temptation to get overly technical here, but in Greek, when the Bible refers to God in the *absolute* sense, it is preceded by an article "*the* God."[2] In John 1:1 when we read that "the Word was God," in our English Bibles, the article before "God" in that clause is not there in Greek. Rather, *the* God is who the Word was *with* and in this text, the Word not referred to as *the* God himself. So, the Word in John one could technically be God in a derivative sense. Thinkers in the Greek-speaking world knew that, so John 1:1 did not suffice as a prooftext for them.

This is a real problem for exegesis when the trump card in any popular-level modern debate over doctrine goes something like this: "Show me one Scripture, chapter and verse, that explicitly says _____. Oh, there isn't one? Then your view is unbiblical and must be rejected." The speaker here presumes to have won the debate because their opponent did not provide explicit prooftexts. If Arius insisted that Athanasius prove himself in that same way, Athanasius would not have been able to point to a chapter and verse that explicitly says that Jesus is ὁμοούσιον (*homoousion*): "of one being/substance with the Father." Yet, this is an essential affirmation for Christian thought. In fact, it's so central that to be unable to affirm this is to not be Christian in the historical sense. In spite of its essential nature, there is no "chapter and verse" in the Bible that says this explicitly. *This central Christian dogma can only be seen with an imagination formed by Christian worship.*

---

2. In John 1:1, *the* God = τὸν Θεόν (*ton Theon*).

THE "BIBLICAL" FOUNDATIONS OF BAD TEACHING

One biblical text that became a major point of contention in the crucial argument over who Jesus is in relation to the Father, is a surprising one—at least in our modern context. The text in question is Proverbs 8:22–25.[3] It reads:

> The Lord *created* me at the beginning of his work, the first of his acts of long ago. Ages ago I was *set up* (established), at the first, before the beginning of the earth. When there were no depths I was brought forth, when there were no springs abounding with water. Before the mountains had been shaped, before the hills, I was brought forth (begotten).

If I were to ask you who the first-person pronouns are clearly referring to in this passage, you would likely check before and after this cited text for clues to tell you who the historical author intended the speaker to be. As it turns out, the author does indeed identify the speaker as wisdom (v. 1), and verses 4–36 consist of what she, wisdom, cries out while standing beside the city gates (v. 3). So, for the modern reader, there's not much controversy here. This text simply has to do with what wisdom, if she were personified, would be crying out beside the gates of a city. And in application, we would perhaps exhort hearers of the text to live wisely by heeding her instructions. Harmless enough. However, in early Christian debates, there was much that needed to be discussed here. Indeed, how one read this text delineated the difference between orthodoxy and those who would deny it.

Allow me to first note the point of agreement. Both sides of the debate about Jesus's divinity agreed that the speaking subject in this text, who is explicitly identified as wisdom, was none other than Christ himself. The wisdom who is speaking is the Logos, the Son of God, Jesus of Nazareth. This should not come as a surprise

---

3. Hans Boersma has written a powerful and lucid book on patristic biblical interpretation. It has been a gold mine in the writing of this chapter and I wholeheartedly recommend it for a deeper study on this and other matters related to how early theologians read Scripture. See Boersma, *Scripture as Real Presence*.

considering that for the early church fathers, the point of reading Scripture is to encounter Christ. Accordingly, all Scripture was written about him, pointed to him, spoke of him, and—historical authorial intent notwithstanding—he himself was the speaker of Scripture.

Given that Christ as the speaker was assumed, we now come to recognize why verses 22–25 came to be a problem. If Jesus is speaking in Proverbs 8, Arians can point to this as yet another clear prooftext for their position. Jesus is outright saying that the Lord created (⬚κτισεν) him, set him up or established (⬚θεμελίωσεν) him ... before the beginning of the earth. Is this not fully resonant with Christ as the firstborn over all creation as Paul clearly teaches? Does this not suggest the Arian position that Jesus was a special creature, lower than the Father but elevated over other creatures, through whom all of creation was brought into being? Finally, does this not make sense of the words of the incarnate Christ himself where he seems intent to assert his subservience and lack of equality with the Father, as we just noted above?

What I find particularly interesting is the basis for the arguments that came out of the Arian tradition. As is very common in Bible teaching today, they championed a "plain" reading of Scripture while dismissing the allegorical and sacramental kind of reading employed by orthodox Christian thinkers.[4] The difference between orthodox and heretical thought here is not that one camp has a "high view" of Scripture while the other holds to a "low view." They are both taking Scripture seriously and engaging it in the construction of their arguments. Therefore, the battle between these schools of thought lay on the field of their methods of biblical interpretation. The Arians produced many Scriptural prooftexts to defend their doctrinal position. More to the point, they wanted to restrict all discussion on these matters to what can be grounded

---

4. Athanasius was not the only pillar of orthodoxy combating the heterodox teaching championed through a plain reading of Scripture. Gregory of Nyssa was having his own battle with Eunomius, who argued that a literal reading of this very text in question demanded a radical subordination of the Son to the Father (see Gregory of Nyssa, *Contra Eunomium*, 3.1.25–26, 33, *en passim*).

in the Bible alone. The Arian method and manner of reading Scripture was in alignment with the earlier "gnostic" detractors of Christianity that I discussed in chapter 2. However, the context of Scripture for the first theologians of the Christian church was the worship in the churches founded upon the apostles.

ENTER ATHANASIUS

Due to the limited scope of this book, I cannot trace the entirety of Athanasius's arguments and insights. Given that he is a pillar of Christian orthodoxy who does not share the methods of reading Scripture that we are used to today, what I will do here is first show how Athanasius read Proverbs 8:22–25 in his debate with the Arians. I will also note some of his principles of interpreting Scripture against their "plain reading" of Scripture. Related to his reading of this text, I will also briefly sketch Athanasius's two major theological breakthroughs, which end up serving as foundational for how Christians came to recognize the unity of the Godhead.

Let's begin by observing how Athanasius reads Proverbs 8:22–25. Given that this text refers to Jesus, Athanasius insisted that to read the problematic "created me" and "established me" verbs in a way that aligned with Christian worship, was to first inquire into the *person* who is speaking. What is the nature of this person, Jesus? Remember, Athanasius already knew who this person was because through the rule of faith, Jesus is identified, named, and worshiped as the risen one, and to encounter Jesus by the power of the Holy Spirit was to be joined to the Father by that same Spirit. That act of human invocation (calling upon the triune God), and the grace of God to meet us in worship, is our salvation. For Athanasius, the person who is at once fully God and fully human is the one speaking in Proverbs 8.

Against the "plain" reading of this passage, Athanasius denies that it is referring to the origin of a *created* wisdom before time. Instead, Athanasius insists that the intended meaning lays hidden (*kekrymmenos*) in the fully God and fully human person of Christ, revealed in the New Testament and engaged in Christian worship.

The person of Jesus in the New Testament's witness put the God who saves on full display, and he is the now-revealed hidden meaning of Proverbs 8. Proverbs 8 is speaking about God-with-us, and only when read with those assumptions can we discern how to read it as faithful Christians. This is especially necessary considering what Jesus is speaking in verses 22–25.

If Jesus is the person who fully joins us to God, then he simply cannot be "created" in the way we mean "created" in its "plain" sense. The logic of worship and salvation impose upon us limits of how this text could be read. Whatever "created" and "established" mean, they cannot mean that Jesus is a creature who once did not exist. Despite Jesus saying in this text that "The Lord *created* me at the beginning of his work . . . Ages ago I was *set up (established)* . . . Before the mountains had been shaped . . . I was *brought forth (begotten)*," he cannot mean what it "plainly" says because it would mean that Jesus is denying his co-eternality and co-equality with God.

For Athanasius, only an ecclesiastical mind (*dianoia*), or a mind shaped by church practice, can read Scripture as a Christian. Athanasius looks for the "ecclesiastical sense" (church sense) of Scripture and contrasts it against the "private sense" of the Arians. What distinguished Christian thought against heretical thought was not that one was using Scripture while the other was not. Nor is it that one had a "high view" of Scripture while the other one had a "low view." Rather, what distinguished a heretical reading of Scripture from a Christian one started with the lenses through which Scripture was read. Athanasius is confident that his interpretation is right because he has received insight into the "mind" of Scripture through the rule of faith received from his predecessors. Athanasius does not isolate any biblical passage at hand from the lens received through the church's christological convictions.

Athanasius's First Breakthrough: (Re)Reading Proverbs 8:22–25

Athanasius sought to read this text as a worshiper of the triune God who saves us in Christ. How ought we as Christians read the voice of Jesus saying that God created him (v. 22), and established him (v. 23)? It was questions like this that pushed Athanasius to one of his major theological breakthroughs (breakthrough one of two that will be discussed here) that made Christian readings possible for other difficult passages such as this. Athanasius taught us that when reading Scripture, we must discern when it is speaking of God's *internal* (or immanent) life, and when it is talking about God's *external* (or economic) acts toward creatures.

There are times when Scripture gives us explicit insight into God's internal life. For one example, when Jesus is alone praying to the Father, he asks the Father to "glorify me in your own presence with the glory that I had in your presence *before the world existed*" (John 17:5). God has an internal life that is eternal and preexists creation, and Scripture speaks of that reality as the glory shared between the Father and the Son. Having said that, the private life of God is also consistent with his public acts for the sake of the world. Continuing this example from John 17: because the Father and Son share glory in their internal life with one another, the Father and the Son analogously share glory in their external life toward their creatures—"The glory that you have given me, I have given them, so that they may be one, as we are one" (John 17:22). Who God is and what he shares for his own sake is what God does externally *for our sakes*. Hence, the point of sharing his glory is "I in them and you in me, that they may become completely one, so that the world may know that you have sent me and have loved them even as you have loved me" (John 17:23). To recall a point made in previous chapters, God is not anxious about inhering in and identifying with creatures, even at cost to himself.

The basic principle of interpretation is this: sometimes Scripture speaks of God's eternal/private life shared between Father, Son, and Holy Spirit. Other times, Scripture speaks of the triune God's saving acts/public life toward creatures. The internal and external acts of God are consistent because they flow from the same triune life. Discerning the difference between the internal and external life of God in Scripture can get tricky when talking about Jesus. After all, he is God the Son (the eternal Logos), and

Jesus of Nazareth (the historical man) in one person. Therefore, it takes a churchly trained mind to read Scripture and discern when it is speaking of God's eternal/private action, and when it's speaking of God in Christ acting "for us and for our salvation."

To chart this out for clarity: when Scripture speaks of Jesus, because he is simultaneously Jesus of Nazareth and the eternal Son of God, Christian interpreters of Scripture are to discern when the bible is speaking specifically about:

- The eternal Son of God who preexists creation with God (John 1; Col 1; Heb 1); and
- The incarnate Jesus who "for us and for our salvation" fully assumes all of humanity and lives as a creature.

With this insight in mind, Athanasius offers two readings of Proverbs 8:22–25.

Reading one: Keeping the distinction between the internal and external life of God in mind, Athanasius argues that because Jesus says that the Lord has "created me for his works" and "established me," Jesus is talking about his external incarnate life in verses 22–23. The "for his works," part of the text notes that what Jesus does when incarnate, he does *for* and *as* creatures. God creates and establishes Jesus incarnationally for us and for our salvation. For Athanasius's first reading of this text, Jesus is "created" and "established" incarnationally for us, so that we might be in him and so joined to the Father.

Continuing with Athanasius's first read of the text, verse 25 is less of a problem for Christian theology. It uses the language of "begets" or "brought forth" in reference to the Christ's relationship to the Father. For Athanasius, this simply refers to the eternal life of the triune God. The Father eternally begets the Son. For the Father to be the *eternal* Father, there must be a co-eternal begotten Son for him to be eternally begetting. Otherwise, there would be a time where God was not Father, making him a non-eternal Father. Later, we will learn that the Spirit is the very act of eternal begetting. Hence Father, Son, and Spirit are co-eternal, living one shared life.

To recap Athanasius's *first* engagement with Proverbs 8:22–25:

- God's external life: The "created me" and "established me" verbs that Jesus uses to describe his relationship to the Father refer to Christ speaking as the incarnate Jesus.
- God's private life: The "beget me" verb refers to the Son's eternal relationship to the Father.

Reading two: Athanasius returns to this passage later and will offer a second reading. Despite the differences, I want the reader to note how both of his interpretations of Proverbs 8:22–25 can be faithful to Christian thought and practice because both will retain the divinity of Jesus. Notice, the question isn't, "What does the Bible 'plainly' teach," but "Does what is 'plainly' seen in Scripture align with Christian dogma of who God is and how he relates to creatures?"

Regarding his first engagement with the passage, Athanasius grew uncomfortable with splitting the external life of God (vv. 22–23) and the internal life of God (v. 25) in verses that are so close in proximity. He would still apply the principle of discerning when Scripture speaks of the private life of God versus the economic life of God to his reading. However, in his second reading of the passage, he opted to follow the lead of a predecessor, Origen of Alexandria. Athanasius agrees with Origen, who says that all of these verbs ("created," "established," and "beget") reveal the work of the eternal Son of God. For Origen, the "created" and "established" language refers to the founding of creatures *in* the Son. The Son *precedes* creation. As both the Alpha and Omega of all that is, Christ is both the foundation and the fulfillment of creatures.

Regarding humanity, Genesis says that we are made in the image of God. That said, we also know that the image of the invisible God is none other than the Son himself (Col 1:13, 15). Because Jesus is eternal, that means that humanity as personified by Adam was made in the image of the Son who is the quintessential image of the invisible God. Notice, the predicates Scripture uses for humanity and for the Son are identical—but because the Son is God, he always precedes us. Therefore, through Christ, humanity as the image *from the beginning* is created to share in the eternal wisdom and knowledge of the Son.

How does identifying the speaker of Proverbs 8:22–25 as the eternal Son of God illumine this passage for Christians? What could it mean for God the Son to say "you created/established me" to the Father? We can only understand this once we overcome our temptation to be pious by keeping God separate from creatures.

The Bible says of Jesus that he is the image of God. It also says that of human beings. Jesus is the image of God in the absolute sense, and humanity is in the image of God because and only because it is "in him that we live and move and have our being." In the Son's identity with creation, Jesus saying to the Father "You created/established me" is not a problem for Christian orthodoxy. That is because humanity being made in the image of God means that predicates that used to be understood as only belonging to creatures ("created/established"), can now be understood as being true of God. God truly and actually assumes humanity *for our sakes*. Doing so does not make him less God, but it makes creatures more like him. That is to say, it divinizes us. Once again, who is it in Proverbs 8:22–23 that says to the Father "you have created . . . established me"? *It is none other than God-with-us; it is none other than God the Son with humanity speaking as one person.*

This reading accomplishes many things: First, it deals a powerful blow against the Arian reading of this passage using the church-sense of Scripture over and against a "plain" sense. Second, it now understands these few verses to be referring to one person—the Son identifying with humanity—without need to divide between the internal and external life of God in verbs that are so close in proximity. Third, it provides not only the basis for a coherent understanding of the Father's oneness with the Son, but also of the oneness of creatures to the Son—and so our oneness with the triune God. Augustine will later come to call Christ joined to the body by one name: The total Christ (*totus Christus*). Fourth and finally, it sets the powerful groundwork for orthodox Christology.

Athanasius's Second Breakthrough: Worshipfully Reading Scripture

We have just noted one of Athanasius's major theological breakthroughs: Scripture speaks of the internal and external life God. When talking about Jesus, readers must discern when Scripture is highlighting the internal or external life of God while always noting that these works are not divided among separate persons. God the Son and the incarnate Jesus are the same person. And by God's benevolence, we can now be identified with that one person.

What about Athanasius's other theological breakthrough? It goes as follows: If we are to trust that our being joined to Jesus truly saves us—that is, if we are to trust that being joined to Jesus in worship is what joins us to God—then Jesus must be God to the same degree that the Father is God. Why? Because if Jesus isn't fully God, then our knowing of Christ and our being joined to Christ in worship cannot be said to be a full joining to the God who saves. If Jesus isn't fully God, then there is indeed a "gap" between him and the Father at the various levels we just spelled out above. How might Athanasius respond to the explicitly biblical gaps—of knowledge, goodness, and will—between the Father and the Son as explicated in the words of Jesus himself?

Knowledge: The Father knows things that the Son does not.

- "But about that day and hour no one knows, neither the angels of heaven, nor the Son, but only the Father" (Matt 24:36)
  - In light of Christian worship, Athanasius might say: The Son must know God *fully*, or else we cannot trust anything he says about the Father. In order to fully *know* God, Jesus must fully *be* God.
  - An orthodox reading of this text: Jesus takes on the creaturely (un)knowing of God. In so doing, he doesn't lower his knowing of the Father, but elevates our knowing of

God by making it possible for us to share in his knowing more fully.

Goodness: The Father is good to a degree that the Son is not.

- "Why do you call *me* good? No one is good except God alone" (Mark 10:18; Luke 18:19).
  - In light of Christian worship Athanasius might say: The Son must be God (in goodness and nature) in the same that the Father is God because whatever the Son might lack of God's nature, so too our salvation would lack. We must be able to trust that an encounter with Christ is an encounter with the God who saves. If Christ lacks God's nature in any degree, then when Christ is present with us in our worship, we as creatures are being joined to another creature (idolatry)—one who is less than God. Therefore, our salvation is in question.
  - An orthodox reading of this text: Jesus takes on creaturely goodness, which when compared to that of God, is deficient. In so doing, he doesn't lower his goodness below that of the Father, but elevates our goodness by making it possible for us to more fully share in his.

Wills: The Father can will things that the Son does not. At the garden of Gethsemane, their wills are not only different, but at odds.

- "Not my (Jesus's) will, but your (the Father's) will be done" (Luke 22:42; Matt 26:39 *par*).
  - In light of Christian worship, Athanasius might say: The Son and the Father must perfectly share the same will, so that everything Christ does and teaches both reveals and simply *is* the will of God.

- An orthodox reading of this text: Jesus takes the will he shares with humanity and the will he shares with the Father into the garden of Gethsemane. By being obedient, he submits the will of humanity to the will of the Father. In so doing, he doesn't lower his will to that of creatures below the Father, but elevates the will of creatures to reconcile and at-one our will with his. (This gets worked out more thoroughly in the centuries to follow, especially via Maximus the Confessor).

"God Became Man That Man Might Become..."

Notice that to understand the unity of the Father and the Son the way that Athanasius (and subsequent Christian thinkers) does demands an imagination formed by Christian worship of the triune God, and to consistently follow through by reading Scripture considering that formation. God gives himself to be present to us. His presence in us is our salvation. God identifying himself with creatures doesn't make him less God, it elevates creation to be more like him. Hence the New Testament language of new creation. Being joined to Christ deifies us. That is our salvation. This brings us back to Athanasius's famous line: "God became man that man might become god."

Nor was this a novel idea then, or unique idea since. This is simply a clear and concise statement of that which was taught before him and continued to be taught after him. It is a teaching that makes sense of and displays the radical importance of the relationship between the triune God and creatures. Below, you will find a list (not exhaustive) of important Christian thinkers who have all said—in their own unique ways—that God's aim is to deify creatures:

Irenaeus of Lyons (c. 130): "Because of his infinite love he became what we are in order to make us what he is himself" (*AH* 5. *Praef.*)

Gregory of Nazianzus (c. 329–390): "In Christ that which assumed and that which was assumed are both God" (*Or.* 37.2)

Basil the Great (c. 330–379): "Just so are the Spirit-bearing souls that are illuminated by the Holy Spirit: they are themselves made spiritual, and they send forth grace to others. Thence comes ... understanding of mysteries, apprehension of secrets ... unending joy, remaining in God, kinship to God, and highest object of desire, becoming God" (*On the Holy Spirit,* 9).

Gregory of Nyssa (c. 335–395): "In the one case he is united to us insofar as he sustains existing things. In the other case he united himself with our nature, in order that by its intermingling with the divine it might become divine ... Contact with the divine power acts like fire and effects the disappearance of what is contrary to nature." (*Cat. Or.* 25–26).

Augustine of Hippo (c. 354–430): "He who justifies is the same as he who deifies, because by justifying us he made us sons and daughters of God ... If we have been made children of God, we have been made into gods" (*Exposition of the Psalms* 49.2).

Maximus the Confessor (c. 579–662): "God became man in order to save lost man, and ... to fulfill the great purpose of God the Father, recapitulating all things, both in heaven and on earth, in Himself, in whom they also had been created" (*Ambigua* 41, pp. 109, 111).

Thomas Aquinas (c. 1225–1274): "For just as it is impossible for anything to set fire but fire, so it has to be God alone to divinize, by sharing communion in the divine nature by means of the participation of a sort of assimilation" (*ST* 1–2.112.1).

Martin Luther (c. 1483–1546): "By faith the human person becomes God" (*in epistolam S. Pauli ad Galatas,* 182); "The righteousness of God ... is the righteousness by which God is righteous, so that God and we are righteous by the same righteousness, just as by the same word God makes us be and we indeed are what he is, so that we may be in him and his being may be our being" (*WA* 2, 259:11–14).[5]

---

5. Both *via* Jenson, *Systematic Theology,* 2.297.

Conclusion

In the early church, the triune God was so explicitly worshiped that it raised crucial theological questions about the one God who is present with his creatures. This illustrates that, when done faithfully, Christian worship, prayer, theology, and reading Scripture cannot be separated. Athanasius was a quintessential model of a theologian who read Scripture in light of the logic at work within Christian worship. What emerged from his methods are nothing less than what we now know to be basic Christianity. God is Father, Son, and Holy Spirit; in Christ, God has joined himself to creatures and has deified them by the power of the Holy Spirit through Christian worship. These basic convictions gave him the ability to discern the mind of Scripture. He read it as a Christian formed by church practice.

Sadly, despite him being a pillar of orthodoxy, his insights and methods seem strange to us. We have become comfortable referring to "God" in an *ad hoc* fashion as singular monad—a being among beings. We don't discuss theology trinitarianly, nor do we explicitly worship and name God as such. Trinitarian language has all been lost in our formation and only matters when we're asked to check some doctrinal boxes by the gatekeepers. Moreover, we seem to imagine that our private reading of Scripture saves us from deception. In the next and final chapter, I will sketch how and why the Trinity got moved from the center to the periphery as we imagined that our private readings of Scripture can save us from deception. This will also highlight how and why orthodox teaching about the God-world relation sounds foreign to us. I pray that this will inspire a turning back toward the triune God-with-us.

CHAPTER 8

Out with the Old, Forward with the Ancient

As you therefore have received Christ Jesus the Lord, continue to live your lives in him, rooted and built up in him and established in the faith, just as you were taught, abounding in thanksgiving.

—COLOSSIANS 2:6–7

It is permitted for those who share in the mysteries to investigate with awe and to wonder at the economy of God, and the riches hidden and concealed inside the outer form of the words of Scripture.

—ISAAC OF NINEVEH, HEADINGS ON SPIRITUAL KNOWLEDGE

FOR THE ATTENTIVE READER, perhaps Part II of this book has raised a nagging question. *If it is true that Christian formation happened through Christian worship of the triune God via the rule of faith, and if it's true that the rule of faith was vital for engaging the triune God, salvation, and her Scriptures—why have all explicit forms of the rule of faith been absent from popular church expressions today?* Answering this question will occupy us in this final chapter. I will do so by identifying three different shifts that took place in Christian thought and practice. These shifts happened in:

1. The definition of the "rule of faith" (from trinitarian worship to Scripture by itself).
2. The understanding of salvation (from happening by way of being joined to God, to happening through mental assent).
3. The understanding of God (from the triune infinite act of existence, to a separate and discrete being).

THE SHIFT IN THE "RULE OF FAITH"

As a reminder to the reader, in a previous chapter, I identified the "rule of faith" as a set of speech habits and practices that formed the worship life and thought life of the earliest Christian communities. These practices and habits created and incubated a "culture" where Christians were formed by the triune God who was named, identified, and worshiped for his saving acts in and among them. The rule of faith later developed into fixed texts that we now call Christian creeds. To abandon creeds, then, is to abandon something crucial at the heart of early Christian formation.

Abandoning the rule of faith and creeds would come to leave a gap in the Christian imagination. As tends to happen in all living communities, when something essential leaves it, something else will inevitably fill that gap. Throughout the early church followed by the patristic and medieval periods, what was formerly a marriage between habitual worship practices *and* Scripture, later got collapsed into Scripture all by itself. After the medieval period—following the Renaissance and Humanism—the rule of faith went through that gradual shift.[1] Put simply, Scripture by itself became the only rule of faith. This would later create the problems that we have inherited in today's Christian practice.

---

1. Due to restrictions of space, I cannot lay out the full details here; nor would the intricacies be particularly helpful for a more popular audience. For some literature on this shift (and I intentionally choose authors from Protestant traditions) see Vickers, *Invocation and Assent*; Allert, *High View of Scripture?*; Jenson, *Canon and Creed*; Thomassen, ed., *Canon and Canonicity*. I must note my indebtedness to Vickers in particular for how this chapter is shaped.

When Scripture alone became the sole rule of faith, it eventually decentralized the role of community in Christian formation. Now, the individual reader under the guidance of the Holy Spirit could know God and discover who he is by simply reading Scripture by him or herself. For this to work, it had to be asserted that Scripture was clear and sufficient. I need only to remind you of the debates I sketched in the last chapter between orthodox thinkers and those who opposed them to show why this is a bad assumption. It is also worth repeating here that the difference between orthodox and heterodox thinkers wasn't that Christians had a "high view" of the Bible while the heretics had a "low view" of it. Rather, it was that Christians were reading and hearing Scripture within the context of—and as a people formed by—Christian worship (via the rule of faith) while the others imagined themselves to be following a "plain" and private sense of Scripture.

THE MISAPPROPRIATION OF SCRIPTURE ALONE

There is a popular slogan that has been misused for far too long in the church today. It is a slogan that has led us to glory in our individual power of discernment. That slogan is *sola Scriptura*. In this case, I am using that slogan in its popular understanding. It goes something like this: the Bible, the Holy Spirit, and the "individual" Christian reader alone are all that are needed to discern truth. In an attempt to discuss this responsibly, I am going to be explicitly engaging the arguments of a Lutheran theologian. That is because it was primarily the Lutherans who originally championed the slogan.

Robert W. Jenson (1930–2017) was a Lutheran theologian whose life's work was aimed at reconciliation between Protestants, Catholics, Orthodox, and those from the various free church traditions. He was convinced that the only theology worth writing was that which was for the sake of a unified and holy church. Annoyed that it was often misappropriations of Lutheran phrases that people weaponized for the sake of happily colluding with disunity, Jenson wrote a little book called *Lutheran Slogans: Use and Abuse*.

For Jenson, one such slogan that is now being abused is indeed *sola Scriptura*.

Jenson says that the word *sola*, or, "only" is meant to exclude other things. But when the Catholics asked if by *sola*, the Lutherans meant Scripture and *not* creeds, the magisterial Reformers insisted that they did not mean that. Nor can "only" mean to exclude church leaders and teachers (the episcopate). The reason being is that the New Testament and the establishment of church leaders emerged as a joint response to the same problem. The crisis I am referring to is that at about the year 150, the original apostles and their disciples had died off. Therefore, the church could no longer simply ask them for clarity when a theological issue or questionable teaching emerged. What the church had to do in response was collect apostolic writings as touchstones of the true gospel message. The gathering and establishing of these New Testament texts were done by none other than church leaders. Therefore, "it was an episcopally governed church that acknowledged the canon. If the New Testament was a gift of the Spirit at a crucial time, why not the episcopate (church leadership) that received the gift?"[2] Jenson concludes that using *sola Scriptura* to deny the church's ancient governance is indeed an abuse.

So far, for our Lutheran friend, the *sola* in *sola Scriptura* cannot mean Scripture and *not* creeds, nor can it mean Scripture and *not* church leadership. For we need both creeds and church leaders to help us read Scripture faithfully. Finally, Jenson wants to insist that this slogan cannot mean Scripture and *not* tradition. This should go without saying, but Scripture did not fall from the sky in one leather-bound book. Rather, it is itself a collection of documents that were gathered by human collectors for the sake of preserving the gospel tradition. "If we have no confidence in tradition under the leading of the Spirit, we can have no confidence in supposedly inspired Scripture . . . Thus the rule that the writings there collected are authoritative for the life of the church is itself a pure piece of churchly tradition."[3]

2. Jenson, *Lutheran Slogans*, 66.
3. Jenson, *Lutheran Slogans*, 66.

I must remind the reader that this is not a Catholic or Orthodox theologian engaging in debate or polemics against Protestants. This is a Protestant combating the misappropriation of slogans that emerged from his own tradition. To put the final exclamation point on the folly of pitting Scripture and tradition against each other, I will simply let Jenson have the last word:

> The use of *sola Scriptura* to enforce "not tradition" is thus a mere oxymoron, [which] has done widespread damage in the life of the Protestant churches, fostering the delusion that we could ignore centuries of theological reflection and debate . . . without loss of access to Scripture itself. The church received the New Testament as a controlling part of her tradition, not as a substitute for it . . . The difficulty is that Scripture is a book, and thus cannot itself exert its own authority; someone must do this.[4]

I THINK, THEREFORE I AM SAVED

The misappropriation of *sola Scriptura*—especially from those movements that went beyond and came after the magisterial Reformers—meant that Scripture bore a new weight from those who read it. Following the Reformation and the advent of various academic movements (like humanism and its accompanying philology), Scripture gradually began to function differently for Christians. Its primary role moved from being a way in which we prayerfully and sacramentally encounter Christ, to being understood as a reliable source of true knowledge. The effects of this are still with us today, as I cannot go a year without hearing a sermon or teaching on "the reliability of Scripture." To be clear, the early magisterial Reformers had been formed in a church context that still centralized the worship and doctrine of the Trinity. Therefore, they still taught and explicitly worshiped the triune God early on. But the shift from the rule of faith being understood as that which identifies the triune God who saves us, to Scripture by itself, would start to have a profound impact on the church.

4. Jenson, *Lutheran Slogans*, 67.

Jason Vickers—a Protestant theologian—has pointed out that this shift was especially pronounced and solidified during the seventeenth-century English Reformation.[5] Prior to the sixteenth and seventeenth centuries, Christian practices had a very long and rich tradition, and those who participated in them had the assurance that through this worship, they were joined to the triune God who saves. The shift to Scripture alone as the sole rule of faith created a pastoral crisis that shook worshipers to their core. The new existence of a rival (Protestant) church with its distinctive vision of sacraments and salvation created an existential problem. The truth about God and about where and how salvation was available to human beings was at stake.

Notice how salvation—which meant being joined to the triune God—was once connected to the full giving over of the *whole* self. This is why it was so deeply connected to embodied communal worship. It involved all the senses: touch (laying on of hands), taste (eating the body of Christ), smell (incense), the material world (water, oil, food), and involved human love and desire (worship and affective encounter with the living God). It was in and through these embodied, formative, and heart-orienting acts, that (to recall Origen) the divinity of God resides and finds a place among us. As we pointed out in chapter 7, the glory of the Lord that fills heaven and earth can also fill that which was built by human hands (2 Chr 7). By the time we arrive to the seventeenth century in England, all these salvific acts of worship have been displaced. Salvation moved from being understood as being joined to the triune God through embodied worship, to being saved by "believing" rightly as "faith" came to be understood as mental assent. In technical terms, salvation went from doxology to epistemology.

To claim that "believing" safeguards us from "works righteousness" is yet another abuse of a Lutheran slogan, according to Jenson. "Indeed, believing as a condition I have [to] fulfill is

---

5. As mentioned above, I must point to his important work: Vickers, *Invocation and Assent*. Another important work also cited therein, is Abraham, *Canon and Criterion*.

of all 'works' the most frustrating and irrelevant."[6] Beyond its irrelevance it can be sinful in that it negates the *promise* of the gospel by turning it into a *law* with a condition of belief.

> When I hear "Only believe!" ... I cannot help asking "but ... can I believe?" Or perhaps I am less reflective and simply set out to pump up some belief. Either way I turn in on myself, which is the very thing meant by "works-righteousness"; indeed it was Luther's general definition of sin (to be sinful is to be *incurvatus in se* "turned in on oneself").[7]

Despite the irrelevance and sinfulness of turning "belief" into a work of mental assent, Vickers points out that during the time of seventeenth-century English Protestantism, this understanding of how one got saved was solidified. Moreover, "faith" in God (as just described) seemed to mean something more like faith in the reliability of the Bible. "Humans must simply give their 'full and firm assent' to those things contained in or deduced from Scripture in order to secure their salvation by faith. In a fateful moment for English Protestant theology ... '*This assent is called faith*.'"[8] Vickers goes on to point out that "instead of salvation having to do with the invocation of the triune God ... in worship, thanksgiving and praise, it now had to do with the cognitive rational activity of giving assent to propositions contained in or deduced from Scripture."[9] By giving mental agreement to these propositions and the *certain* truths found in Scripture, individual Christians were thought to be able to attain the assurance of the most infallible kind.

Scripture itself, and the individual knower of Scripture displaced the church's worship of the triune God as principal for salvation. Given the new weight placed on Scripture and the knower of Scripture, it simply *had* to be asserted that "God had made Scripture utterly *clear* and *plain* with regard to the things

---

6. Jenson, *Systematic Theology* 2.293.
7. Jenson, *Lutheran Slogans*, 11.
8. Vickers, *Invocation and Assent*, 45.
9. Vickers, *Invocation and Assent*, 45.

pertaining to salvation."[10] Considering Arius's pushback against Athanasius noted in the previous chapter, the words "clear" and "plain" should be cause for pause. This left the leaders of English Protestantism to determine which doctrines can be more easily deduced from Scripture and assert those to be "essential for salvation" because they are "clearly" found in Scripture.

Considering the many centuries it took for Christians to work out the doctrine of the Trinity while reading Scripture in such a way informed by the rule of faith (ecclesiastical sense), the assertions of the English Reformers would spell disaster for the doctrine of the Trinity. Church history shows that the doctrine of the Trinity is not accessible through a plain reading of Scripture, unless it is read with a mind formed by Christian worship. This is why by 1650, the classic doctrine of God was on its way to being displaced. "Given that Scripture as the rule of faith was now pivotal for the assurance of personal salvation, it would be difficult for any English Protestant to imagine giving it up. This was true even when the commitment to *sola Scriptura* threatened the doctrine of the Trinity."[11]

Throughout the rest of his book, Jason Vickers shows the various arguments raised by thinkers after the English Protestant Reformation. They refused to budge from the principle of Scripture alone as the sole rule of faith, while also trying to prove that a Christian understanding of the Trinity could be found in "clear" biblical propositions through a "plain" reading of Scripture. Long story short, their efforts left much to be desired at best and were disastrous at worst.

I spend time talking about the English Protestant Reformers because I can't help but see how we have essentially adopted their principles and slogans despite the glaring shortcomings. We too demand that Scriptures be simplistic and reliable. The main difference is that they were at least attempting to make sense of the triune God, while we seem to see no reason to be bothered to make any efforts at all. We are content to tell people: repeat a

---

10. Vickers, *Invocation and Assent*, 49.
11. Vickers, *Invocation and Assent*, 57.

prayer asserting your belief in God, read Scripture by yourself and for yourself while attempting to do what is says. Practice this for a lifetime, and you're squared away. The doctrine of the Trinity, incarnation, the presence of God in the world, and the effects of resurrection can all be reserved as matters for the church's intellectual elite. Let those remain as topics important to the classroom, but not the church.

I want to close this section, once again, with a quote from our Lutheran friend I have been citing in this chapter. I mentioned that when something gets removed from Christian thought or practice, it creates a gap that we will then have a need to fill with something else. The gap that was left from doing away with the rule of faith as it was classically understood was to put new pressure on the Bible to *be* something for us. It *had* to be reliable, perfect, and errorless. It *had* to be clear. It *had* to be simple. It *had* to be sufficient in and of itself. The certitude of our salvation by way of mental assent depended on it. These newfound "necessities" were guaranteed by a certain understanding of God's "inspiration" of Scripture by the Holy Spirit. But this habit of thought, says Jenson, is:

> A disastrous false start that might even be regarded as sinful: we have gone at the matter of Scriptural inspiration backward. We have begun with what we think we need from Scripture (e.g., its reliability & clarity), and then have recruited the Spirit to assure us that our supposed needs are satisfied. But since the Spirit in question is *God* the Spirit, we must not in quite this fashion tell him what to do. Surely, we must rather start with the doctrine of the Spirit, with what we know of his character and work, and then ask to what ends this particular Spirit would have provided the church with the Scripture we in fact have, and how he would have gone about this provision. *That is, our reflection needs to find its base in the doctrine of the Trinity*; moreover, we should not be offended if a Spirit so identified disappoints some of our desires.[12]

---

12. Jenson, *Inspiration of Scripture*, 7–8 (emphasis mine).

THE GOD-WORLD RELATION CHANGES

Finally, in answering the question of why the rule of faith and the doctrine of the Trinity have been decentralized in the popular expressions of the church today, I will close my reflections by noting the shift in the understanding of God and how he relates to creation. Without the rule of faith to form the church to read Scripture as Christians ought, Scripture was read in light of other influences. As I mentioned in chapter 1, we don't know ourselves by ourselves. We are formed by how we relate to our families, friends, and our broader cultural, institutional, and societal context. If the church doesn't form me to worship, act, and read as a Christian worshiper of the triune God, I will come to the text not unformed, but formed as a member of other given contexts.

This is what makes insisting on the clarity of Scripture particularly dangerous. What Scripture "plainly" says according to one context with its given methods of interpretation can differ significantly from another. The cultural factors of my day will always play a part in my imagination as I read Scripture. This is partly why church is not optional for the Christian. I continue to participate in the worship of the triune God in a church that continues to form me despite the assumptions that the world is trying to form me to hold. The Christian church forms me to know God as the triune God with us, for us, and in us. The risen Jesus alters how I understand a creation tending toward *new* creation. Only when reading Scripture in that light can I claim any meaningful attempt to read Scripture as a Christian.

To recall a crucial point from chapter 3, in the classical doctrine of God, God is not a being among beings. He is the I AM: the Infinite Act of Existence in which all other creatures live and move and have their being. God is not another discrete item or agent in a world that consists of items and agents. He's not a being that has love, he *is* the Love that makes it possible to love at all. The true love I have for my family does not happen outside of God; rather, faithful love shared between creatures is understood as finite participations in the infinite wellspring of Love that exists between Father, Son, and Holy Spirit.

A God so understood in classical Christianity also carried a vision of his relation to creation. Between God and creatures there was a *real* and *intrinsic* connection—a real sacramental link between God and creatures. For classical Christian thought, there is no such thing as nature ungraced or untouched by God. There was not this one thing called created nature that was designed to get along without God, and then this other thing that is a God who could add or withhold his life from creatures. There is no creaturely existence "outside" of God.

God creates what we call nature *out of nothing*. Therefore, there is no such thing as self-sufficient nature. After all, what is nature but that which is always already utterly dependent on God and other creatures to be itself? A blade of grass participates in the existence graciously given by God, and is utterly dependent on dirt, oxygen, water, the earth, and the cosmos to be itself. When creation is understood as always dependent on God, the word "creation" does not name an action of God in the "past." God is as actively creating right now as he "was" in Genesis 1 and 2. The classical understanding of the word "creation" is that it names the ongoing relationship between God and creatures. It's a relationship whose fulfillment does not happen until the creation that God calls forth from nothingness is *fully* joined to him. It is in him that we live and move and have our being, always. But in the end, creation will be "completed" and fulfilled in Christ when he is "all in all." When creation is understood as the continuing act of the triune God, and headed toward fulfillment in him:

> There is no abiding difference within one gift of both creation and deification; there is only one grace all the way down and nature all the way up ... Creation, incarnation, salvation, deification: in God, these are one gracious act, one absolute divine vocation to the creature to become what he has called it to become. To exist ... is simply to

have heard and (from the very first instant) responded to this total vocation.[13]

It is no surprise that the same community that understood God to be so inherently intimate with creatures would also read her Scriptures sacramentally. They read it as a word from Christ in the words and writings of humans. The question was not *whether* Christ is being spoken of or speaking in a given text, but *how*. Understanding the ubiquity of God in Scripture naturally followed from understanding the ubiquity of God in all things. I gave a very brief description of how the rule of faith was displaced, but how was the picture of God's inherence in all things displaced in the Christian imagination? That question will occupy the final section of this chapter.

DISENCHANTING CREATION

Some of the explicit ideas that caused the shift of understanding God as the one in whom we *truly* and *actually* "live and move and have our being," to an abstracted being among beings who is extrinsic to the world and rules only from above it, are as follows. First, God had to be removed from nature and humanity. There was a long movement of many factors that contributed to this, but it became explicit with a Scottish priest named Duns Scotus (c. 1265–1308). He was deeply resistant to the classical articulation of the Creator and creature relationship through the doctrine of analogy. The doctrine of analogy simply says that whatever belongs to God infinitely, analogously belongs to creatures according to our finitude. The Beauty that God is and the beauty that we experience are analogous. We experience finite beauty, but that's only because Beauty itself exists infinitely in God. The beauty of sunsets awakens creatures to Beauty itself. Creature and Creator remained distinct because whatever was true of God naturally, was true of creatures derivatively. God remains God, and we remain utterly dependent on him.

13. Hart, *You Are Gods*, 19–20.

Back to Scotus. Rather than the existence of creatures being understood as directly borrowed from the existence that God is, Scotus preferred to say that God has his own being, while creatures also had their own being. God's "being" and our being got severed. God could now be said to exist as an item among items, and a being among beings. In this picture of reality, you have *a* being called God, and beings called creatures. This raises the question that if the being of God and the being of creatures are understood in this similar fashion, what makes God *the* God over creatures? This posits God and creatures in sort of ontological rivalry. The interaction between God and creatures would inevitably fall into the zero-sum rivalrous game that I have been resisting throughout this whole book.

If God and creatures were no longer *actually* linked, what was it that joined God and creatures? Within this new vision of the God-world relationship, the answer was simply, "God's will." Things no longer have to *actually* be true, rather, God can *arbitrarily* will something to be so, and it is so. It used to be that what made God *the God* (and not a god or creature) was that he was the Infinite Act of Existence: Goodness itself, Truth itself, Being itself who graciously went forth in creation.

Now, God's sheer will is what distinguishes him as God. "Good" can mean one thing for God, and something completely different for creatures simply because God wills it. "The consequences were close at hand: if something is good strictly because God *wills* it to be good, then couldn't God declare anything, even the most horrible act, to be good? Now, it seems, there is nothing in almsgiving itself that makes it an inherently good act; God simply wills and declares it to be so."[14]

It is often supposed that God can do this because we're so depraved as creatures that we can't possibly know what good is. This is exactly what I mean when I say that, in this picture of the God-world relationship, God must relate to creatures in a zero-sum game. God's knowledge must be set *against* ours. God's goodness must be set *against* ours. God's glory must be set *against* ours.

---

14. Boersma, *Heavenly Participation*, 77.

God can do as he wills *against* our will. So that the knowledge of God, the goodness of God, the glory of God, and the will of God can, *and mostly does*, come at the cost of creatures.

However, despite our sin, creatures can still *know* what good is. We can still inherently know a good act from an evil one. We can still know what it means to be a good father who gives good gifts: "if you being evil know what it is to give good gifts . . ." The relationship between God's good gifts and our good gifts is not at odds, but analogous . . . "*how much more* will your Father in heaven give good things to those who ask him." The word "good" analogously means the same thing for God and creatures. Simply stated: we are indeed allowed to draw analogies between words that apply to God and creatures. They are limited in scope but significant in their ability to speak truthfully. Hence, God's giving of good gifts and being a good father cannot mean the *opposite* of what it means for us, but much *more*.

WHAT'S IN A NAME?

Once God was understood as a discrete being who was abstracted from creation and can thus do as he wills over and against creatures to assert his God-ness, a man by the name of William of Ockham delivered the final blow to the classical picture of God and his relationship to creatures. In the ancient world there was an understanding that universal concepts of good, beauty, truth, humanity, and felineness were categories that described real things. In other words, I know what *a* human is, because I have a sense of what humanity is. I can know true things because there is a real category of Truth. William of Ockham found these universal categories unnecessary. Universal categories, says William, are simply names and that we as creatures assign to things that look alike in order to make sense of our world. He was so committed to cut off the world of transcendence from our creaturely one, that he had no room in his imagination for transcendent categories whatsoever.

This raises the question, if "humans" do not share in "humanity" so that you and I belong to a same transcendent and universal category called "human," what then is it that connects us? Ockham's idea severed our connection with one another. Moreover, without being connected to transcendence of any kind, we have also been cut off from any real connection with God. This would have profound impact on understanding our connectedness to God and each other, which is the same thing as saying that it would impact theology.

Think of the impact on classical Christian teaching. Christians have asserted that in Christ, the triune God assumes *humanity*. This meant that what Jesus accomplished in his humanity is made accessible to all humans. If you cut off the universal concept of humanity, how could Christ's assumption of humanity matter for human beings? Once individuals are severed from God and each other, the answer became once again, the will of God.

The overall picture this creates is this: God is separate from creatures as a discrete being over and against other beings who also do not share a real connection. God can act in a world cut off from him if and how he so wills. His "holiness" and "sovereignty" means that he is so utterly *separate* from us that he can be "justly" cruel and call it good, if he so wills. God's *Godness* is no longer found in that he is the I AM, the triune God in whom we live and move and have our being, who benevolently gives of himself to at-one himself with creation at his own cost; neither is he the Life of Love shared between Father, Son, and Spirit who is always True, Good, and Beautiful. In this new disenchanted and disconnected world, God is now an abstracted, single, monadic, gigantic being whose Godness is displayed by his sheer power, authority, "sovereignty."

When the God-world relationship is imagined in this way, and there is no classical understanding of the rule of faith to reform it, what becomes "clear" in Scripture starts to shift. As demonstrated above, the doctrine of the Trinity becomes hopelessly obscure. God *is* Love changes to mean that God is a being who has love and can choose to withhold it, if he so wills. Everything, even God's love, submits to his will and power. Is not Scripture "clear"?: Jacob have I loved, Esau have I hated. God can be understood to "slay us" and we are pious when we respond, "though he kill me, yet I will trust in him" (Job 13:15). That is, until our piety runs out and we cry out in protest, only to be met with: "Where were you when I laid the foundations of the earth?" (Job 38). Or better, "Who are you to argue with God . . . has the potter no right over the clay?" (Rom 9:20–21).

A "plain" reading of these texts allied to a zero-sum God just described would suggest that a creature is pious to the degree that she or he submits to equivocity without protest. Equivocity means that words that apply to God and words that apply to creatures can mean and be experienced as opposite realities. Scripture applies the predicates of "just," "merciful," "wise," and "truthful" to God, so we are obliged to believe that those are true of God in some way. But for the Christian who subverts all predicates of God under his "sovereignty" and power, God can will them to be experienced as the opposite of what they mean for humans, and we simply are to submit.

As John Stuart Mill has pointed out: "To say that God's goodness may be different in kind from man's goodness, what is it but saying, with a slight change of phraseology, that God may possibly not be good?"[15] If our claims about God oblige us to use words in a way that makes the divine meanings of words and creaturely meanings of words antithetical, then the predicates become equivocal. Indeed, if our words are *that* contradictory to the truth of God's love, then all Christian and creaturely language is semantically and syntactically meaningless. Nor does insisting on the human intellect's "total depravity" do anything but restate the problem. If our minds are that depraved so that we can only trust a "plain" reading of Scripture for our salvation, what are we doing adopting methods of discerning the truth in biblical texts that are the same as discerning the truth of secular history books as taught by the academics of our culture? Scripture does not give us a method of interpreting itself. So then, why would we trust "depraved" minds to give us methods for how to read it?

---

15. Mill, *Examination*, 128.

CONCLUSION

Neither this chapter nor this book is ultimately about biblical interpretation. There is much more that can be, and indeed, has been said on the matter. Rather, this chapter was about identifying the shifts that took place in Christian thought and practice that decentralized the classical understanding of Father, Son, and Holy Spirit, and how that impacted the way Christians understood creation in relation to her God. Once these shifts took place, Scripture seemed to "clearly" affirm the novel vision of "God" that came to be assumed.

These shifts have lived out their logical conclusions in popular church expressions today, and we seem to be trapped in a disenchanted world while worshiping a distant and monadic god. Such a "God" can relate to creatures only in terms of a zero-sum game. The more pious among us are the ones who in an effort to "take Scripture seriously" (by the methods we've received) imagine that "God's" glory, sovereignty, and holiness are put on full display when they come at the cost of creatures. Moreover, the more pious among us simply submit without protest and demand others do the same. Equivocity is thus fully embraced.

But I can't help but note the difference between this posture, and the posture held by those who so radically thought according to the more ancient understanding of the rule of faith. Church fathers such as Ignatius of Antioch, Clement of Alexandria, Origen of Alexandria, the Cappadocians, and Maximus the Confessor, among others, refused equivocity. These thinkers are premodern, so their rejection does not stem from a kind of modern sensibility to make God out to be "nice." Nor is it based on biblical ignorance.

Origen notes these following texts that puts anger, punishment, regret, and evil at the hands of God: "A fire has been kindled from my anger," (Deut 32:22; Jer 15:14) and "I am a jealous God, repaying the sins of the fathers upon the children unto the third and fourth generation" (Exod 20:5) and, "I regret that I anointed Saul to be king" (1 Sam 15:11) and, "I am God, who makes peace and creates evil" (Isa 45:7) and again, "There is no evil in the city which the Lord has not done" (Amos 3:6) and, "Evils came down from the Lord upon the gates of Jerusalem" (Mic 1:12), and "An evil spirit from God tormented Saul" (1 Sam 16:14).

Origen is aware of these texts and rejects the notion that they should be read as literally applying to the God revealed in Christ. For Origen, this misappropriation can only happen when one applies their understanding of justice without recognizing that Jesus reveals God as good. Christ, Origen says, "proclaimed to us a more perfect God." Those who don't see Jesus as the key to the full revelation of who God is, ascribe evil to God because a "plain" reading of Scripture demands that they "believe such things about him as would not be believed even of the most unjust and savage human beings." In other words, if you read of God acting in such a way that you would recognize as evil in a creature, then you're not interpreting Scripture faithfully.[16]

Notice, Origen does not suggest that it is our understanding of good and evil that is mistaken, it is that our reading of Scripture is. He, like most of his Christian contemporaries and those who followed him, read Scripture allegorically, looking for Christ at every turn. The point of Scripture is to encounter Christ. Thus, Orthodox theologian and priest Fr. John Behr has gone so far as to say on a multitude of occasions: "If you aren't reading the Scriptures spiritually or allegorically, you aren't reading them as gospel." These minds worshiped God via the rule of faith. Through a centuries-long process of thinking in light of said worship, and reading Scripture spiritually, a faithful understanding of the doctrine of the Trinity and his relationship to creatures emerged.

Perhaps, then, it is high time we move out with the old, and forward with the ancient. Perhaps, then, we should pay attention

---

16. Origen of Alexandria, *On First Principles* 4.2.2. Nor were the fathers just mentioned Marcionites. Marcion of Sinope was excommunicated from the church around 144 for rejecting the Old Testament as Scripture precisely because he read it in literalist fashion, which in those days, was a deviation. The move the fathers made was to receive the Old Testament as an occasion to see Jesus in them when properly read. Therefore, the fathers did not reject the Old Testament but received it with special care taken as to how it was to be interpreted.

to the thought and life of the church that gave us the very Scriptures we rightly privilege in our own lives and practice. It seems to me that therein lies deep treasures to turn away from our disenchanted world of flux where we are severed from God and each other. May we turn to these sources as we seek to discern the triune God-with-us in the days ahead.

Conclusion

As Jesus is on his itinerant mission, he arrives at the region of the Gerasenes where he is immediately encountered by a man who is so insane that he lives "among the tombs and on the mountains . . . howling and bruising himself with stones" (Mark 5:5).

As the scene plays out, we see a man trapped in a world of torment wrought by a multitude of lying voices. He is waiting on the shore for Truth himself, Sanity himself, Love himself—Jesus of Nazareth. There's something about the soundness of mind that is deeply attractive for those being tormented by agents of insanity. No one knew the name of this man. Those in the city referred to him as "the demoniac." But this will not do for Jesus. To get at the core of this man's identity Jesus asks, "What is your name?" The response that came out of the demoniac revealed that his identity had been disintegrated. The lies of a multitude of voices had reached his core. He was no longer a sane one, but a host of fragmented identities: "My name is Legion; for we are many" (Mark 5:9).

Jesus sets the man free without contest. But what I find incredibly revealing in this story is the reaction of the onlookers. "They came to Jesus and saw the demoniac sitting there, clothed and in his right mind, the very man who had the legion; and they were afraid." A once howling and self-harming man sits with a soundness of mind next to Jesus, and *this* is what provokes fear in the witnesses; "Then they began to beg Jesus to leave their neighborhood" (Mark 5:17). Truth comes at a cost to any culture that is accustomed to insanity, so they ask Truth to leave.

This story serves as a sobering illustration of what seems to be going on today. I sincerely wish that in relaying the untethered confusion of the demoniac that I was merely describing the conditions of the world that have wrought insanity on the people trapped in it. All I'd have to do is simply exhort the church to continue to be the embodiment of Truth that draws the tormented to bow to the Prince of Peace. But it seems that today, the church itself has been subjected to a legion of voices telling us who we are. We somehow have become just as susceptible and vulnerable to the anxiety, dread, and confusion of the world. I can't help but think that it is now *us* to whom Jesus is asking, "What is your name?"

Our inability to answer Jesus's question with any kind of coherence exemplifies a problem that this book has hoped to address, at least in part. As argued, persons are formed by their surrounding world. People know themselves by how they relate to others, and the ways in which others relate to them. In our (post) modern world, culture tacitly (and even explicitly) communicates to me that my identity is self-made and discovered privately, all by myself. This is not a Christian option. However, given the way that we practice Christianity individualistically, the members that make up the body have no recourse but to construct an identity that counters the one given to me by culture. Imagining that my individualistic reading of the Bible safeguards my identity is merely a restatement of the problem.

My prayer is that this book encouraged you to recognize that there are deep and formative reasons that the church has survived as long as it has, despite the legions of voices and threats it has encountered throughout its two thousand years of existence. This is no accident. The steadfastness of God's people, however imperfect, is connected to its intentional formation by the Spirit, rooted in a recognition of who she is in relation to her active God. This was never a smooth or easy process, yet she remains in existence today, nonetheless. The church remains with the same call: creating communities that live by the promises granted to creation through the resurrection of Jesus. Christ is risen. In a world where we still

CONCLUSION

see death and decay, we construct our identities by the reality that death does not have the final say.

I have shown that communities are ways of constructing human identity. The church has known this and has lived its life and practiced its worship accordingly. The church "exists because God has acted and continues to act in a certain way. The church exists because it claims this action of God is a process of reconstructing the entire human race."[1] This is anything but a boring and inconsequential claim. A community so understood, then, cannot afford to be held captive by Legion for too long.

The world has its working or assumed definitions of what it means to be human. This will always be the case. The church must reckon with and counter it when necessary. This is what it means to be a public and communal witness. In its mission, the church has a specific challenge: "making sense of itself in the light of the claim that God has acted and still acts, and the claim to the reconstruction of humanity . . . The world will always ask 'Why should anyone listen?' and the answer to that question isn't provided by a Church that is struggling to be fashionable and intelligible at all costs, but by a Church that lives and speaks in such a way that is sharply challenges what the world takes for granted."[2]

This is an audacious claim, but if the triune God we worship is real, it is a claim we must make and live by. Either we as the church show people what it means to be human, or Legion will. Moreover, if we as the church are not diligent about our communal formation, Legion will prey on our individualism and leave us equally confused. We detect lies by knowing the truth. We detect false identities by knowing ourselves in relation to the God who creates and acts in among his creatures. Those tasks begin through reconnecting and remaining grounded in the ancient story of God-with-us.

---

1. Williams, "Authority of the Church," 17.
2. Williams, "Authority of the Church," 17.

Bibliography

Abraham, William J. *Canon and Criterion in Christian Theology.* New York: Oxford University Press, 1998.
Allert, Craig. *A High View of Scripture? The Authority of the Bible and the Formation of the New Testament Canon.* Grand Rapids: Baker Academic, 2007.
Aquinas, Thomas. *Summa Theologiae: Prima Secundae, 71–114.* Vol. 16. Edited by John Mortensen. Translated by Laurence Shapcote. Green Bay, WI: Aquinas Institute, 2019.
Athanasius. *On the Incarnation.* Translated by John Behr. 44B Popular Patristic series. Yonkers, NY: Saint Vladimir's Seminary Press, 2011.
Augustine of Hippo. *Expositions of the Psalms.* Nicene and Post-Nicene Fathers: Second Series 8. 2nd ed. Edited by Philip Schaff. Peabody, MA: Hendrickson, 2012.
Balthasar, Hans Urs. *Love Alone is Credible.* San Francisco: Ignatius, 2004.
Basil The Great. *On the Holy Spirit.* Translated by Stephen M. Hildebrand. Popular Patristic Series 42. Yonkers, NY: St Vladimir's Seminary Press, 2011.
Boersma, Hans. *Heavenly Participation: The Weaving of a Sacramental Tapestry.* Grand Rapids: Eerdmans, 2011.
———. *Scripture as Real Presence: Sacramental Exegesis in the Early Church.* Grand Rapids: Baker Academic, 2018.
Congar, Yves. *I Believe in the Holy Spirit: The Complete Three-Volume Work in One Volume.* New York: Crossroad, 1999.
Gregory Nazianzen. *Oration 37.* Nicene and Post-Nicene Fathers: Second Series 7. 2nd ed. Edited by Philip Schaff. Peabody, MA: Hendrickson, 1996.
———. *To Cledonius the Priest Against Apollinarius.* Nicene and Post-Nicene Fathers: Second Series 7. 2nd ed. Edited by Philip Schaff. Peabody, MA: Hendrickson, 1996.
Gregory of Nyssa. *The Catechetical Oration.* Edited by J. H. Strawley. Cambridge: Cambridge University Press, 1917.
———. *Contra Eunomium.* Nicene and Post-Nicene Fathers: Second Series 5. 2nd ed. Edited by Philip Schaff. Peabody, MA: Hendrickson, 2012.

Hart, David Bentley. "God, Creation, and Evil: The Moral Meaning of *Creatio Ex Nihilo*." *Radical Orthodoxy: Theology, Philosophy, Politics* 3.1 (2015) 1–17.
———. *You Are Gods: On Nature and Supernature*. Notre Dame: University of Notre Dame Press, 2022.
Ireneaeus of Lyons. *Against Heresies*. Ante-Nicene Fathers: Second Series 1. American ed. Edited by Alexander Roberts. Peabody, MA: Hendrickson, 2012.
Jenson, Robert W. *Canon and Creed*. Louisville: Westminster John Knox, 2010.
———. *Lutheran Slogans: Use and Abuse*. Delhi: ALPB, 2011.
———. *On the Inspiration of Scripture*. Delhi: ALPB, 2012.
———. *Systematic Theology: Volume 2, The Works of God*. Oxford: Oxford University Press, 1999.
MacIntyre, Alasdair. *After Virtue: A Study in Moral Theory*. Notre Dame: University of Notre Dame Press, 2007.
Martin, Lee Roy. *The Unheard Voice of God: A Pentecostal Hearing of the Book of Judges*. JPTSup 32. Blandford Forum: Deo, 2008.
Maximus the Confessor. "Ambiguum 41." In *On the Difficulties in the Church Fathers: The Ambigua,* edited by Nicholas Constas. Vol. 2. Cambridge, MA: Harvard University, 2014.
McKnight, Scot. *Kingdom Conspiracy: Returning to the Radical Mission of the Local Church*. Grand Rapids: Brazos, 2016.
Mill, John Stuart. *An Examination of Sir William Hamilton's Philosophy: And of the Principal Philosophical Questions Discussed in His Writings*. London: Longmans, Green, and Co., 1889.
Moore, Rickie. *The Spirit of the Old Testament*. JPTSup 35. Blandford Forum: Deo, 2011.
Origen. *Contra Celsum, Book IV*. https://www.newadvent.org/fathers/04164.htm.
———. *On First Principles*. Edited and translated by John Behr. Oxford: Oxford University Press, 2017.
Robles, Ray C. *Theological Metaphysics: A Pentecostal Theology of Being*. London: T&T Clark, 2024.
Schafroth, Verena. "An Exegetical Exploration of 'Spirit' References in Ezekiel 36 and 37." *JEPTA* 29.2 (2009) 71–73.
Sonderegger, Katherine. *Systematic Theology: Volume 1, The Doctrine of God*. Minneapolis: Fortress, 2015.
Stronstad, Roger. *The Prophethood of All Believers: A Study in Luke's Charismatic Theology*. Cleveland, TN: CPT, 2010.
Thomas, John Christopher. *He Loved Them Until the End: The Farewell Materials in the Gospel According to John*. Cleveland, TN: CPT, 2015.
Thomassen, Einar, ed. *Canon and Canonicity*. Copenhagen: Museum Tusculanium, 2009.
Vickers, Jason, E. *Invocation and Assent: The Making and Remaking of Trinitarian Theology*. Grand Rapids: Eerdmans, 2008.

Williams, Rowan. "The Authority of the Church." *Modern Believing* 46.1 (2005) 16–28.

———. *Being Human: Bodies, Minds, Persons.* Grand Rapids: Eerdmans, 2018.

Zizioulas, John. *Being as Communion.* Crestwood, NY: Saint Vladimir's Seminary Press, 1985.

www.ingramcontent.com/pod-product-compliance
Lightning Source LLC
Chambersburg PA
CBHW031338160426
43196CB00007B/711